OTHER SCHOOLS
OF
THOUGHT

OTHER SCHOOLS
OF
THOUGHT

Morris Panych

Vancouver   Talonbooks   1994

Published with the assistance of the Canada Council

Talonbooks
201 - 1019 East Cordova St.
Vancouver, British Columbia
Canada V6A 1M8

Typeset in Palatino and printed and bound in Canada by
Quality Color Press Inc.

First Printing: June 1994

Rights to produce *Life Science*, *2B WUT UR* or *Cost of
Living*, in whole or in part, by any medium by any group,
are retained by the author. Interested persons are request-
ed to apply for permission to Patricia Ney, Christopher
Banks and Associates, 6 Adelaide Street East, Suite 610
Toronto, Ontario, M5C 1H6. For amateur production
rights, contact the Playwrights Union of Canada, 54
Wolseley St., Toronto, Ontario, M5T 1A5.

Canadian Cataloguing in Publication Data

Panych, Morris.
  Other schools of thought

  ISBN 0-88922-346-7

  I. Title.
PS8581.A65O83 1994   C812'.54   C94-910116-8
PR9199.3.P325O83 1994

CONTENTS

PREFACE

I had no intention of writing three plays when I began working on *Cost of Living*, but even as I began developing that piece there was rekindled in me a certain spark of youthful rebellion. I remembered my institutional education and all that I longed to learn about life and all I didn't learn in that environment. I believe I was denied, through my teachers and through their system, the opportunity for true self-realization. I don't deny that my education gave me a certain academic knowledge, but it was hopelessly superficial. My sexuality, my identity, my feelings, my lack of faith, were never addressed. And like all young people, I wandered through my early life in fog.

Through these plays I had a chance to replay, in an imaginary way, the years I had missed living; the days and months of inexplicable sorrow and confusion that I had endured the way most young people endure them — in solitude and silence. I wrote these plays as much for adults to reflect on their past as for young people to reflect on their future.

Although there is a specific educational aspect to these plays, I view them as deeply personal. In writing these characters and their situations I found an emotional attachment that was entirely unexpected.

I asked Ken MacDonald, designer for all three original productions, and my long-time collaborator, to describe briefly each set as it first appeared. These descriptions are not meant to discourage other scenic approaches, but are given only to provide these pieces with a clear visual context for those readers who may not have seen the plays performed live, and who wish now to imagine them as they were presented. The visual presentation of my work is central to it. It's why I like to direct my own plays, initially. The practical realization of the play is as important to me as the written material — as informative, and as necessary. To invent plays on paper is only the starting point of a whole integrated process.

§

I dedicate this book to my dear friend and colleague Larry Lillo, who passed away last year after a long and noble battle with AIDS. His story, more compelling and meaningful than I could ever write, will always inspire me, and many others, to bring honour and dignity to our lives by accepting things as they are, while valiantly fighting for what they should be.

Morris Panych

PRODUCTION NOTES

LIFE SCIENCE

Because of the need for projection screens, the set was simply two large framed rectangles with rough-cut black wooden frames. Each frame was mounted on a metal stand with casters, so they could be moved around to create different looks. Newsprint sheets, which could be written on or used as projection screens for EDNA's photos, were stapled to the frames. EDNA could also tear off pieces of newsprint when needed to create an interplay with the photos, or the shapes that projected parts of photographs. The idea was to show, by example, what creative things one could do with very little in the way of technology.

2B WUT UR

As this production played in a theatre, and did not tour, we went for different values here — an enormous head, twenty feet high, sprouting two musicians out of the top. The set was like a building construction site: The head was only half built, partially exposing the interior framework. The idea was to show a person in the process of trying to form his own identity. Other construction-site aspects were brought into play and doubled as the locations in which the play takes place: Lockers represented the school, and on occasion CAB's parents appeared from two manholes.

COST OF LIVING

Once again, we wanted to show how a high school student could put together an interesting and creative environment in which to express himself — in this case, with the use of video. We built a welded frame on which were set eight TV monitors, painted on or around. In front of the monitors was a table with the VCR and a tape-deck for the music. To one side was a bar stool and a music stand for graphics, and on the other, two life-sized, naked mannequins. There was also a video camera, with which the actor could take live shots of both himself and the audience. Everything was to have a made-up, impromptu feel about it, as if quickly thrown together for a class presentation.

Ken MacDonald

PRODUCTION CREDITS

Life Science, *2B Wut UR* and *Cost of Living* were all commissioned and first produced by Green Thumb Theatre for Young People, Vancouver, B.C.

§

Life Science premiered on September 30, 1993, at Templeton Secondary School, Vancouver, B.C., with the following cast & production team:

EDNA   Ellie Harvie

ACTORS IN SLIDES:
MOM   Patti Allan
WENDY   Margaret Barton
RALPH   John Ormerod

DIRECTOR: Morris Panych
SET & COSTUME DESIGNER: Ken MacDonald
SLIDE DESIGN AND PHOTOGRAPHY: Tim Matheson
COMPOSER: Greg Ruddell
HEAD CARPENTER: Tim O'Gorman
PROPS & COSTUME ASSISTANCE: Elana Honcharuk
STUDY GUIDE: Theresa Goode
STAGE MANAGER: Carolyn Reemeyer
TECHNICAL ASSISTANT: Chris McGregor

§

2B WUT UR premiered on April 9, 1992, at the Vancouver East Cultural Centre, with the following cast and production team:

CAB	Alex Ferguson
MOM/CAROLINE	Patti Allan
DAD/DEEK	Ian Ross McDonald
DEWEY	Veena Sood

DIRECTOR: Morris Panych
SET & COSTUME DESIGNER: Ken MacDonald
LIGHTING DESIGNER: Gerald King
MUSICIANS: John Mann, Hugh McMillan
SOUNDTRACK PERCUSSION: Vince Ditrich
SET CONSTRUCTION: Bruce Timko
HEAD COSMETIC DESIGNER: Michael Wolski
PROPS & COSTUMES: Val Arntzen
STAGE MANAGER: Michael Miciak

In the original production, CAB's Songs were written and performed by John Mann and Hugh McMillan of Spirit of the West. They are available on request by contacting Janet Forsyth, c/o Suite 506 - 119 West Pender St., Vancouver, British Columbia, V6B 1S5

§

Cost of Living premiered on September 28, 1990, at St. George's School, Vancouver, B.C., with the following cast and production team:

OUR GUY   David L. Gordon

ACTORS IN VIDEO:
GUY IN WHEELCHAIR   Ken MacDonald
DAD   Patrick McDonald
TEACHER   Tim O'Gorman
ANGEL   Karen Olender
MOM   Meredith Bain Woodward

DIRECTOR: Morris Panych
SET & COSTUME DESIGNER: Ken MacDonald
VIDEO DIRECTOR: Tony Papa
STEEL FABRICATION: Paul White
PROPERTIES: Val Arntzen
STUDY GUIDE: Theresa Goode
STAGE MANAGER: Nina Richardson
TECHNICAL DIRECTOR: Gavin Bakewell

Li[Fe]
SC$_2$IENC$_1$E

Margaret Barton as Wendy. *This image was one of those presented in* Edna's *slide show in the Green Thumb Theatre production of* **Life** Science. *Photo by Tim Matheson.*

Music. A series of black-and-white slides,
depicting young people at a wild party. These
are operated with a certain hard-edged
purposefulness by EDNA, *a very serious young*
woman in a short skirt and a big baggy sweater;
she is, in other words, a budding intellectual. A
picture of herself is the last to appear. She stands
in front of it, and applies bright red lipstick as
she speaks.

EDNA
These are . . . people . . . I know.

Having fun.

I'm in that crowd somewhere.

If you look real close you might just be able to pick me out.

That's me. Edna.

You could never picture me, without picturing the whole crowd.

> *She applies lipstick to a picture of herself on the*
> *screen.*

> *The lips remain while the picture changes, so*
> *that the lips are worn by different of people.*

Life is an ordinary kind of thing. After all — everybody has one. It's easy to forget you're alive. Until someone pinches you. Or the tires of a car squeal *(Sound of squealing*

3

brakes) and death comes to a sudden, an abrupt stop just a fraction of an inch from you, as you're making your way across some busy street — on your way to science class some morning.

You might stop for a moment to consider the hard, red metal bumper resting just against your thigh, you might pause to consider how others around you would have resumed their life journey, even if you hadn't, you might turn back to consider death for a moment, but in the next moment you continue on your way, like I did, as the red car passes.

He gives me a look, the driver, a look of fearful realization. His life could have stopped there, too. And changed direction forever. Is it any wonder I take his picture? Who wants to forget what the realization of life really looks like? Because otherwise, I forget. By the time I've gotten to the other side of the street I've already forgotten I'm alive. After all — who wants to be reminded?

I arrive at school. The day hasn't even begun yet and somehow I'm tired. Or is it just the whole idea of "formal education"? That cold edifice. That structure. That imprisonment of thought. The penitentiary to which I've been sentenced for twelve long years. The crime? I knew how to live life, but I couldn't spell it. Add to or subtract from it. Divide it into its phylums and its orders. Break down its chemistry. Find its square root. Its medulla oblongata. Its spine. So I dissected it. And studied it. Until I learned not to be curious about it anymore. Forgot the real questions I was in search of the answers to. Just continued on with it, never once turning back to look at life. Because of that fear of realization. That terror of knowing. How close. How very close death stops.

So when I took the picture home and I developed it, when I looked at that driver, as he looked back at me, when I saw that expression of fear, I knew. We have grown too afraid to live. And I don't mean die. We're all afraid of that. I mean, when I look myself, and think of how I think, I wonder if I think at all, or if that's just too much. If I wouldn't rather just get to that other side of the street. Or never even cross the street at all. Until I'm told.

Told what to feel.

When to feel it.

What to wear.

Who to be.

How to be it. According to the image. That's why I party, I guess. With the rest of my crowd. That's why I consider drinking myself into unconsciousness now, the way my crowd is starting to, because my crowd is starting to. Or smoking myself into a blue haze of bewilderment. It's all a fog anyway.

Confusion ought to be a subject taught at school. Just think how well I would do in it. Confusion 10. Confusion 11. Advanced confusion. I wouldn't have to have the answers, just the questions. Like, why don't I feel happy? The girl in the magazine is. Aren't I supposed to be? Isn't everybody on TV? Happy? Fulfilled? Why is my family so unlike those families? Why do I escape upstairs, and into my room? Surround myself with my photographs and try to figure out what goes where.

5

Meanwhile, my mother knocks on the door. She wonders. "What's the matter, Edna. Are you *stoned*?" I'm not. But this is her way of understanding me when I start to think. When I look at life for what it is. If I was stoned, I wouldn't really do that. I wouldn't really do anything except — smile.

Recently I bought some dope, it's true. I'm not even that interested in smoking it. But my mother has certain expectations of me. Actually, it's my "not" being stoned she should worry about. Instead, she gives me this cold blank stare. I just have to take a picture of it. I just have to be reminded what disappointment looks like. Parents don't know. They forget what life is. Why else would they be so surprised when things go wrong. Edna, I'm so *surprised* at you. Why? The world is full of unpleasant surprises, mother. Earthquakes. Tidal waves. Phys-Ed class. It's nature's way of reminding us about life's precarious balance. But as I said, who wants to be reminded. Everybody just wants to wipe it all away. All my friends do. Flip the page. Change the channel. Have another party. So you put on your party face, and away you go.

I guess it was the red car, and the sound of those squealing brakes, but all day that day, I was feeling so distant and strange. I had a sense that I wasn't even in my own body, and that I was floating around somewhere. Like something in formaldehyde. I could see myself, sitting at my desk. But I wasn't really there. I was watching me dragging myself through my own life. And everything was so automatic. My locker, my books, my friends. And none of it quite real. If I didn't know I wasn't stoned, I'd have thought I was. Maybe somehow I'd achieved a kind of perpetual state of intoxication. It can happen. I took pictures of everything that day. Even the ground. Just to make sure I was actually walking on it.

I left school early, just after lunch, and went to a park. Crossed the street. Walked away from my life, my crowd, for a little while. I've never really gone off on my own. But today — I felt like I was singled out for something. Maybe I just singled myself out. And I entered a forgotten, other world. The one cars hurry through, on their way to somewhere else. Even the wind doesn't stay long here. Rushes past in a wild hurry. Scattering leaves into nervous little huddles. These old guys look out at me from inside their coats. Poor, old rags of men. I don't really care about their poverty, to be honest. They're just shapes to me. Interesting — shapes. To photograph. If I had to feel their suffering, even for a second — no, I don't want to feel that. Sometimes, I don't think I want to feel anything. Not cold, not wet, not hungry, not ever. I'd rather feel nothing at all; look forward to nothing; watch the weather channel. Someone passed me in the hall at school. This was earlier. That morning. Someone passed me and said "I can hardly *wait* for the party tomorrow night." I said "yeah." But then it occurred to me: "What is it I can hardly wait for?" Every weekend it's the same. Isn't it? Same brain-damaged ideas. Same dizzy sensation of having wiped it all away. But aren't we always left with that dry taste of Monday morning in our mouths? *"Hardly waiting"* for next weekend, so we can put ourselves through that same wash-rinse cycle all over again? Or is it that we can hardly wait to act like animals, because being human is just too complex. And it's so much simpler to not even try. Or is it that we want to have fun, and even if it isn't really, even if it's the furthest thing from fun that we could ever imagine, everybody says it is. I mean — that's what it says on the package. That's what it says on TV. You see those beefy guys and their chicks drinking beer and having more fun than anybody ever had in their entire lives. Yeah. I can — hardly — wait.

So I'm in this park, and I'm thinking: "Why isn't life a little more like the ad," and trying to get a picture of this disillusionment, when this guy comes up to me. This young guy. But looking a lot older. Taps me on the shoulder. I jerk around suddenly, he's right there. His head kind of bobbing around on his shoulders. "Wanna take my picture" he says. So I did.

This is my friend. Let me draw you an outline of Ralph. *(She outlines his form.)* Ralph is just a regular guy, of the everyday variety. He has a heart and he has a soul and he has a mind.

The pictures change so that the outline fits other people, some famous.

You recognize the pattern, I'm sure. The shape. Ralph grew up in the regular way. So he says. I bought him a cup of coffee and he told me about it. We sat by ourselves on a bench. I don't know why I wasn't afraid. Life, as I've told you, is a fearsome prospect to me. Full of dark nights, and anger, and insects. Full of madness. I take pictures of what's around me, but I wouldn't live in them. And yet there I was, sitting next to this — guy. I was sure I must be someone else. Maybe I am.

Ralph is kind of stoned-out in aspect. He has a lot of ideas. Some of them strange. He keeps himself covered in dirt.

Likes the way it feels next to his skin. Has a few twigs in his hair. You might expect him to collect things. Scraps, and pieces of other people's lives. But he only saves bits of oddball wisdom. Ordinarily I don't like to get advice from the mentally ill, which is why I've avoided the school guidance counsellor so far. Naturally, Ralph regards all professionals with suspicion. As a qualified manic depressive. He's been prescribed all sorts of strange and powerful drugs, but refuses to take them. He says "here," and he hands me a bottle of — something. "You can have them if you want." Oh. He says that being crazy is better than being nothing at all. Thoughts controlled by chemical manipulation. Ideas stifled. Feelings suffocated. He thrives on feelings. Refuses freezing when he goes to the dentist he says, because, in his words, pain is part of the whole picture. Maybe that's why he thinks I should continue with school. Does he know how mind-numbing *that* can be? He says he wishes *he* had, but looking at him you somehow wonder if it would have made any difference to his life. Bad luck destroyed him. Before the alcohol and the glue and mental disorders. Before the wind wore him down and the weather. Places like this seem to just sit and wait for people. I sometimes wonder if there isn't someplace just waiting for me. A house in the suburbs? Somewhere?

Maybe that's what school is. Preparation. Even the weekend is a preparation somehow. The parties, the mindlessness. Part of the developing formula. Part of the overall — picture. The illusion of a life being fully lived. Adults, I've noticed, have come to accept all this. Shrugged their shoulders. Gone jogging. Signed up for classes. My mother takes a night course. "The Philosophy of Education." I think you graduate when you finally figure out how pointless the class is. Like most things, it self-destructs. Like Ralph. Like life.

I mean, I hate to bring up the fact that we're all going to die sooner or later, but it does have its positive side. Or so I discovered. Or so I was told. Ralph said "Death is something I look forward to in the future." I told you he was odd. I had no idea what that meant. And apparently I wasn't going to find out. The next moment he was gone. I was loading my camera, and when I looked up again, there was this old lady just standing there, in an old coat, smiling strangely at me. I was about to ask her what she wanted, when she pointed over in the direction of the street.

Suddenly I heard that sound, that horrible, familiar sound. The screeching of tires. But this time with an ugly thud. And there he was. Ralph. Thrown about twenty feet into the road. Another car squealed its brakes, and swerved to avoid him. That one didn't even stop. But the driver of the truck did. Gets out starts yelling his head off. I don't think he's really mad, but what else do you do when you've killed someone?

So this is what was waiting for Ralph in the end. And that old lady? It was as if she'd sensed it. Where did she go? An ambulance came. But only to take the body away. I wasn't really sad. I wasn't really anything. I thought it would make an interesting series of photographs.

The photographs are shown in dead silence.

Have you ever run, anxiously, to a fire? Have you ever slowed down as you passed a crumpled-up car on the highway, craning your neck to see inside? Why isn't life the spectacle that death seems to be? That would be one of the questions in my confusion class.

But it wasn't until I started to develop certain thoughts that afternoon. Later, at home, in the darkness and the privacy of my developing room. As the images began to appear, of Ralph, there, in the chemicals. As if I'd never seen the tragedy until now. I began to feel very strange. Almost sick to my stomach. It all seemed so unnatural. And then there was that thing he said about death being something he was looking forward to in the future. I wondered. Was it even an accident? I'm still wondering. And what about his family? And what about his friends? And then there was that old woman?

I was proofing the film when my mother came in. She automatically assumes I'm up to something I shouldn't be. "Who *is* this man?" she wanted to know. "Actually, mother. Who *was* this man." "You're definitely stoned" she said. And she left the room. Suspicious as usual. In a way, I like my mother to think terrible things about me. At least, that way, she's thinking about me. But I wasn't stoned this day. On this day, that began so strangely, and was getting stranger by the minute, I was sensing the world in a different way that I didn't even understand.

I had an idea that someone might want to know what Ralph had said before he died, or maybe what he looked like. Someone who cared. I would give them these photographs and I would tell them that he was okay, in his own way. That he was looking forward, but not too far, into the future. I wouldn't say to what. And that he had a smile on his face. Which is more than you can say for most people when they die. So if that's any indication, his life was a great success. Even if it was a total failure.

I wonder what the expression will be on my face when the time comes. Maybe I won't have one. I know exactly what my mother's expression will be. Surprise. She never quite expects things to happen. When they do, she has a vodka martini. She's always so shocked. Whenever she looks in the mirror. Like she forgot how old she was. "Where did those lines come from" she says. As if twenty years passed by in her sleep one night. A time-lapse. And she was suddenly old. I believe part of the reason she hates me so much is that I take pictures of her that make her look how she really is. And I blow them up and give them to her. She studies them for hours. Trying to understand something that she already knows. "You're getting old, mom." "Someday," she says, "you'll be as old as I am now." "Yeah" I says, "but you'll even be older than *that*." She has another drink.

I think drinking is what old people do to feel young and what young people do to feel older. So why doesn't everybody just act their age? Another question for confusion class.

Down at the police station, which is where I went to ask about Ralph, I explained to them that although I didn't know the guy, I had some photographs his family might like. They checked with the Coroner, where the dead are pronounced. Apparently, Ralph had no connections with anybody. So his body was tendered out to the lowest bidder. Some funeral home. Through the Office of the Public Trustee. That's the way it's done, if you don't have any next of kin. A small service is held. Just in case

12

someone shows up. Like me. When I arrived at the funeral home the following day; this is the funeral home — there was this recorded classical music playing. I don't know if Ralph would have liked it. It was pretty sombre. Not like him at all. Pretty generic. And there were no flowers anywhere. Nothing. So I ran out, and around the corner, where I got a bunch of daisies. They reminded me of him. By the time I came back, that old woman, the weird one from the park, was sitting a few rows from the front. She was wearing the same tattered overcoat and a hat, with a little flower in it. I don't know why I was surprised, but I was. That he had a friend. And embarrassed. About the flowers. Suddenly, they seemed so pathetic. Just then, she turned around. Smiled at me. That same smile. Just like she had the other day. She had this ancient and mysterious face. Like, really old complexion, but underneath, like a child. Shiny blue eyes. A sweetness of expression that almost glowed. She didn't seem sad or anything. So I figure she must have known about Ralph and about his aspirations. She said in a hushed tone "Those are lovely flowers." So I brought them up to the front and placed them carefully down. I took a seat across from her. She said, "Did you know him?" Her little eyes were sparkling. I guess I thought it would make Ralph seem more popular than he really was if he had an extra friend that nobody knew about. So I didn't really answer. "Well. It's good to know he had a friend," she concluded. I whispered back. "I have some pictures . . . if you'd like to see them." "Pictures!" she says. "My goodness." So I showed her all the shots I'd taken the day before. She looked at them all with the deepest concentration, as if she was cramming for a final. I admit that part of me was thinking she must be admiring my photographic artistry. They did have a down-to-earth, kind of Diane Arbus quality to them. I

13

tried to seem professional. "He was a good subject" I said, realizing how callous and cold that sounded, even as I was saying it. "You can have them if you want." I told her, since she seem so fascinated by them. "Me?" she said. "To remember him by." "I'm not sure I even know who he was," she said. So. What was she doing in the park, then? And, come to think of it, why did she point to where the accident happened before it even happened? She smiled and handed back the pictures.

Before I could ask her what I wanted to ask, this guy in a double-breasted grey suit entered. Looked at us both. Nodded. We nodded back. He read out some prayers. He asked if anyone had anything to say. The old lady looked at me, raised her eyebrows — shrugged. I couldn't stand the idea of nobody saying anything. Nobody ever does. And life just goes on and on. So I stood up and I said "Yes. I have something to say." Why did I say that? And the man in the grey suit stepped aside, and I made my way up to the podium, and I spoke. I described what sort of a guy I thought Ralph must have been. I had no idea if I was right or wrong, but then, neither did anybody. Apparently. I made up all sorts of stuff about how he had achieved a kind of inner success. I sort of threw my hands up at the end of it. "That's it." The man in the grey suit gave me an understanding smile, shook my hand, and left the room in a hurry. When I looked over, the old lady had tears in her eyes. I took her picture. Feelings have always fascinated me. From a compositional and photographic point of view. "You spoke of him so beautifully" she said, blowing her nose into a old, yellow hanky. "Almost how he really was." "But I thought you didn't know him," I said. "Well, no. Not to hear *you* describe him." I leaned over her decrepit figure and I asked, "Just who *are* you, lady?"

14

"Well, I guess you could say I was a sort of a grandmother to him," she said, tilting her hat on a slight angle and getting up to go, but I stopped her. "You *knew* he was going to be hit by that truck. What was that?" She turned. "There was always a kind of inevitability about Ralph. Don't you think?" "Actually, he was only an acquaintance of mine," I told her. "You don't have to know a person" she said, making her way to the exit, carrying an old shopping bag. "Individuals come and go, but life stays pretty much the same."

I was walking fast to keep up with her, as she left the funeral home. It was as if she could care less whether I heard what she had to say or not. Suddenly she stopped to pick up an old sock, a man's blue sock, just lying in the gutter. She held it up to the light. "That doesn't mean it isn't interesting." "What isn't?" She continued and I continued after her. Every once in a while she'd stop to look at something, but most of the time, she just charged right along, talking about this thing and that. Searching through garbage. Trolling the streets. "The investigation of things is a particular science," she said, at one point, fishing a pair of old swimming goggles out from a sewer drain, with the aid of a broken violin bow she'd found, "but general rules apply, of course. If you live long enough, you'll probably have seen everything. But then you'll probably be too old to remember any of it." By the time I noticed the day passing, it was nearly past, and she was still walking. Stopping to talk to people she didn't even know. Guys slouched in doorways. "Where are you actually going?" I asked her. "Nowhere" she answered, "wanna come?"

There was the party that night. Maybe I could swing by later, I thought. How life changes. Two days ago I would have just wanted to lose myself in the haze of the weekend, and the crash and rattle of the crowd. But on a late afternoon in the autumn, when I left the funeral of a friend I didn't even know, when the colours of leaves changed forever, when the sky turned its brightest blue, and the streets came alive before my very eyes, I was beginning to wonder. Could there be anything stranger, wilder, is there anything more hallucinogenic, more intense, than an ordinary life when you look at it? I remembered the pills that Ralph had given me. I thought, "What if *life* is the experience *drugs* are supposed to be." "You got a car?" she asked me. And I told her "No," so she says "we'll have to take the bus." So we do. Run down to the corner and jump aboard. "Got any money" she says, and I have to pay for her ride. So suddenly, I'm sitting on a city bus, going nowhere, with the ancient, white-haired woman, wearing a sort of strange little hat on top of her head, with a sad little flower in it.

"If we aren't going anywhere, then what's the big hurry?"

"In case you didn't notice, I'm getting on in years."

I drifted away. Started to daydream. I guess I was watching the world go by, and I was thinking how often I watch the world go by and never really notice it — go by. Suddenly, she pinches me. Hard. On the arm. Ow.

"Why did you do that?"

"Wake up, Edna! Time's a wasting."

Did I even tell her my name?

"People," she says. "Look at them."

"I know. I take pictures of them all the time."

"Pictures? What's wrong with the real thing?"

Then, she started introducing herself, and me, to people who would get on. "Hi. I'm Wendy. And this is my friend, Edna." At first I was embarrassed. But after a while, it was sort of cool. There was this fireman, who was retiring next year and moving to the island. Two gay guys from Burnaby, with a Dalmatian puppy. A woman who lost her child through a miscarriage, but was going to try and have another. We got into an argument with an old war veteran who thought he knew Wendy's sister. The bus driver's name was George, and when he let us off he said goodnight, smiling. We said "Good luck with your night school real estate course." Now I know a bus driver named George. I can't believe it.

Wendy said people are in a constant state of waiting to introduce themselves. I had to believe her. She's been around. Around the world. She met John Diefenbaker once, at a barbecue; whoever he is. She met Pope Pius the twelfth, but she didn't care for him. Once, she sailed to Easter Island all the way from Java. She was even in an airplane crash in the Andes. I asked her if she ever took any pictures of all the amazing things that had happened in her life, and all the people she met. "Life is a science, Edna, in perpetual motion" she said. "How can you take a picture of that?"

We went to this late-night place and had a toasted bagel. Everybody was sitting around having conversations. I wonder now if I've ever really had a conversation with anyone. Maybe my photos are conversations. I showed her pictures of my mother. She said mothers had the saddest job in the world; they had to watch their children grow up. I showed her pictures of my life, and pictures of growing up. I told her about all my friends. Showed her a picture. She said she'd rather meet them, so I told her about the party. Reluctantly. Of course she wanted to go. I knew she would. I told her I was having too much fun to go to a party, but she insisted anyway. I knew how much she would embarrass me in front of my friends. But did I ever guess how much my friends would embarrass me in front of her? Was it because I saw them for the first time through someone else's eyes?

We walked in, and the place was chaos, but not the wonderful, liberated chaos I had always imagined. I shouted, just to get over the noise. "Sorry; this is pretty wild." "This?" she said. "This isn't wild. Have you ever been in the middle of a Zulu war dance? Ever rode a thirty-foot wave in a twenty-foot boat? Ever been to Kuala Lumpur on a Saturday night, during a monsoon? That's wild." "For *us* it's wild," I explained. "That's just because you haven't really *done* anything yet. Gone anywhere. When you do, you won't even remember what *city* this was." I hope not.

I think these pictures just about say it all. If they used these for booze ads, instead of the pictures they do, nobody would ever drink again. If they showed us all the dumb risks we take, when our minds are so warped. When we think we know what we're doing and we don't.

18

When we think we're invincible, but we're not. When we think we'll live forever, and be young, but we can't. The world is so full of lies. Pictures of lives that nobody really lives, and things that could never happen. An adult world of glamorous people, indulging in glamorous things. Beer that makes you macho, cigarettes that make you slim. Pictures composed, not found, of people invented, not real. That's why I need to take pictures. Now I know. People lie. They lie about growing up. Or maybe they just forget. So I'm here to remind them — growing up is complicated and it's weird and it's depressing, and I guess that's the reason we do drugs, and we drink, if we do, even though it makes things even more complicated and weird and depressing. Because we just want to have fun, and someone told us, and we can't remember who, that it would be fun, even if it isn't, and we have no minds of our own, because we lost them. Probably at the mall, somewhere. And that's why we go to parties, because we're zombies, and that's how we meet other zombies. Wendy just shrugs and says "Don't be so judgmental. I did all this once. It's just boring. They'll figure that out. Let's go." Outside, I reminded her that Ralph's life was destroyed by booze. "I thought he was hit by a truck" she says. "Was it a beer truck?" "No," I said. "He was a mixed-up, drugged-out alcoholic." "He was just mixed up" she said. "The drugs and the alcohol came later. People will always find a way to deal with their life. Not everyone is lucky enough to find the right way. Like I said, life is a science, and sometimes the experiment fails. Let the poor guy rest in peace." Ralph doesn't even have a grave. I wonder if anyone will remember him, except us. Maybe nobody's meant to.

After the party we walked for a bit. I thought maybe Wendy was getting a little worn out. Tired. Considering her age. I told her I had enough money for a taxi. "Hell, no" she said. She wanted to be outside, in the cool of the autumn night. To see her breath rise in the air, and dissipate, she said. "I love this time of year. It always reminds me of when I was at school." I told her I hated school. She stopped. "Come to think of it, I hated it, too." We both smiled. I asked if I could take her picture. She said I could remember her without it. She's right. But I took her picture anyway.

This is Wendy. It didn't turn out. I don't know why none of the pictures of her turned out, but anyway I'm glad. How can you capture it? Wendy is the neatest old lady I ever met. I never met my grandmother, but I like to think that she was something like Wendy. Wendy lives life like a scientist. Trying everything, and if it fails, forgetting about it and trying something else. "Ever tried smoking a joint?" I asked her, reaching into my pocket. The dope was gone. I guess I forgot it at home. She just shrugged. "I never found it answered the fundamental question anyway" she said, kicking the pavement with her heels as she walked. "What fundamental question?" I asked. "Why life isn't all it's cracked up to be" she said. "I guess old people have found the solutions," I said. "Sure" she said, "if you can call bingo a solution, I guess a lot of them have."

She showed me this place where she hung out as a kid she said. It used to be a dance hall. They have rock groups there, now, but when she was a girl, they danced the fox trot to big bands. And everybody dressed up and it was a real thing. A real — event. I asked her if people got wasted, like they do now, and she said "Sure they got wasted. We had peer pressure and everything. We even had sex, believe it or not. People made mistakes. It's natural. People fell in love. It's pretty hard to be in the world without actually *living* in it. You're influenced by things. Even the gravity of the moon. The changes of the seasons. Ralph didn't want to be influenced. That was his mistake. He tried to make his life into a dream, instead of an adventure." "You might be wrong about him" I said, showing her a picture I took. "He was looking forward to the future." This is supposed to be a picture of her, looking at a picture of him. This is a picture of me, looking at her, looking at a picture of him. There's more to this picture than you can see here. You can't see me changing. Or how an idea developed within me. A feeling. Like an image in the darkroom. There in the chemicals. Starting at the corners of the paper, and slowly forming. Suddenly it appears and I know what it is. I see myself. And it's me, alone. Apart from the crowd for once. Being who I want to be. Doing what I want to do. Like sitting here. In the still of an autumn night, when I should be hanging out, at a party doing what I always do, because that's what everyone else is doing, and what we've always done, but I'm not. I'm talking to an old lady about the fox trot, and the moon is so full I can almost hear the music. I didn't even take a picture of it. Instead I danced. All along the pier, I danced in the moonlight to an imaginary band. Until I couldn't hear the music anymore. I could only hear Wendy's voice echoing, "Time's a-wasting, Edna!"

I looked around, but I didn't see her. I called but she didn't answer.

She was just — gone.

I looked everywhere. I took a bus across town to the park where I'd first seen her. On the way, I introduced myself to the bus driver, and to a woman, sitting near the back, in an old brown coat, carrying a box of fried chicken. They thought I was drunk, and I told them I wasn't, which made it seem even more like I was. I said goodnight to everyone when I got off, but nobody said goodnight to me. I guess you can get away with a lot more when you're older. That's something I look forward to in the future. When I got to the park there was nothing but old newspapers flapping around in the wind. It was dark. All I could hear was that echo of Wendy's voice in my head, "Time's a-wasting, Edna."

I capture time, Wendy. I don't waste it. I hold life, suspended. Like the pause button on a VCR. I'm trying to explain to myself the inexplicable.

Like, for example, my mother, who, by the time I got home that night, had broken into my room, gone through all my private things, and smoked that dope. Why? In an effort, she said, to understand me. Better. So she's just sitting there. Staring at a photograph of herself. And looking really frightened. "I'm shrinking" she says, in this little girl voice. "Like plastic cling-wrap." "It's because you never smoked marijuana before. By the way, mother, you're breaking the law." She freaked right out of course. Tried to call the police to tell them she wasn't stoned. I stopped her. She even wanted to take one of Ralph's pills. Without knowing what it was. She's so irresponsible that way. I said "Mother, don't worry. I'll take care of you." She became very calm after that. Put her head on my shoulder. Fell asleep. Parents. You really have to watch out for them sometimes. Then the cat sort of climbed on top of her and they both went to sleep. This is a picture of my mother I shall always cherish. Slobbering into her own lap. I call it "Dope Fiend." I asked her if I could submit it to the campaign against drug abuse. She'd like to kill me, but I don't know, I think it's some of my best work. I think I've captured something here. Of the glamour. Not something you'd see in a magazine, but then — they're full of images you'll never see. Not in real life, anyway. They'd never print those. The truth is not as glossy as you sometimes imagined it was. It's more like Ralph. Buried somewhere, no one knows.

It wasn't until two days later that I discovered the photograph. The one Wendy had somehow slipped into my coat pocket. This one of Ralph. Age seventeen. I guess it's no coincidence that he's my age in the picture. I guess she wanted me to understand something about him, or even about myself. Or maybe she was trying to scare me off drugs in some weird kind of way. Like, as if. There's already one screwed-up person in the family, thankyou. Besides, as I said before, it isn't death that frightens me. Anyway, I thought she was supposed to be cool about all that. Who knows with her. The fact is, I've never spoken to her again. Or even seen her. I've gone by the park many times. There's an old people's home across the street. Sometimes, I think I can see her sitting in an upstairs window. I'm not sure. Fading, like an old photograph. Sometimes I think I see her on the bus, alone, or standing on the corner, waiting for a light to change. I can't help looking at people now. And wondering what becomes of them.

I asked my chemistry teacher "What's the right formula for living?" I went to math class, but life still doesn't add up. I want someone to explain the physics of my unequal but opposite reactions. I'm sure the teachers all think I'm stoned. But if I was, I probably wouldn't even wonder. My mother doesn't understand my obsession with the everyday mechanics of my existence. She thinks I'll "outgrow" the need to make a study of life. Instead, she expects me to graduate. From teen delinquency to adult indifference. Disappear into another crowd. A lot of people do. She did. Life dissolves somehow into the future for them.

My old party friends and me are drifting apart now. Ever since the night I brought Wendy around, they don't quite get my sense of — irony, anymore. They think I'm judging them. But I can't judge them without judging me. Besides, there isn't time for that now. I'm taking pictures. I'm saying hello to people. I'm looking at the moon. I'm planning a trip somewhere wild. I'm going out on my own, in search of a few answers.

I'll send photos.

THE END

$$\frac{\frac{2B}{WUT}}{UR}$$

Ian Ross McDonald as Dad, *Alex Ferguson as* Cab *and Patti Allan as* Mom.
Green Thumb Theatre production. Photo by Eike Schroter.

CHARACTERS AND SETTING

CAB, *a young man with a lot of imagination*
MOM
DAD
DEWEY, *a girl who's just "one of the guys"*
DEEK, *another buddy*
CAROLINE, *a party girl*

The play takes place in the no-man's-land of CAB's imagination.

———————

• 1 •

CAB

Sadly, I report that I won't be at school today. I'm giving myself a break because that's just the way I feel.

MOM

Fine.

DAD

That's great.

CAB

You see? They don't care what I do. They think everything's cool — because they're so liberal, and because when they were my age, they had to do what they were told. So — I thought I'd fly down to Vegas, guys.

DAD

Gee. I wish I could have done that when I was your age,
Cab.

CAB

What did I tell you.

MOM

Bring a jacket, Cab. It gets pretty cold in the desert at
night.

CAB

That's okay, Mom. I was just testing you to see how far I
could go. Kids are sort of like dogs that way. That's why
you sort of have to train them. Dogs, I mean. Kids, on the
other hand, should be free to be what they are. Is that
right?

MOM

That's right.

DAD

To be what you are. That's the most important thing in
your life

CAB

Yeah? So tell us about it, Dad.

DAD

When I was your age, I wanted to be a musician.

CAB

No kidding, eh? A violinist, wasn't it?

DAD

A violinist with the symphony. But I didn't do that.

CAB

Why not?

DAD

Because life was different for us, then, Cab. More practical.

CAB

Not like now.

MOM

Now you have a lot more choices.

DAD

It wasn't considered cool to be a violinist then.

CAB

It isn't considered cool to be a violinist *now*, Dad.

DAD

Yes. But now everything is okay. Sort of.

CAB

He never listens to me. This is when he goes off into a
dream. He's starts to pretend he's in an orchestra. He puts
on tapes and plays the violin. That's why the drapes are
always shut at our house. I shut them. Because life here is

so — wide open — that most of the neighbours wouldn't appreciate it. I know I don't.

MOM

Are you having breakfast this morning, Cab?

CAB

I hate this question.

MOM

It's up to you.

CAB

Yes. I know it's up to me. I wish it wasn't. I wish nothing was up to me. I wish I had no choices in life, mother. Especially this early in the morning.

DAD

I thought you weren't going to school this morning.

CAB

But I am going to school this morning. What else is there to do at this time of day on the planet earth?

DAD

You don't have to go to school. School isn't necessarily the only thing you can do.

CAB

I'm aware of that.

Mom

When I was a girl, I wanted to run away and join a clown theatre troupe. I wish I had.

Cab

Mom's a performer. That's where I get my theatrical tendencies from. I know how to become different people when I need to. I can be sad when something sad happens. Laugh when someone tells a joke, even if it's bad. Ha! Ha! See? I can be repentant. Thoughtful. Serious. An incredibly good student when the teacher's looking, and an incredibly bad one when they're not. People like me because generally, I'm whatever they want. Like a menu. Just order. In fact, there's only one thing in life I have any difficulty being. Me.

Song begins.

You hear that? There's a song that goes on inside my head all the time and that's it. A voice that sings to me everything I need to know. It's like way down deep somewhere, someone telling me who I am, so that I can *be* that. But I can never hear it, because there's too much else going on around me.

The Song continues.

• 2 •

Cab

My name in Cab, because apparently I was conceived in a taxi. Or so the myth goes. My parents were the last of the hippies. You know what those are. People who had a generation to live in. An identity. Even if everyone had the same identity, at least they *had* one. But us? We're the lost crowd in the middle of a destination between two points. All my life, it seems, I've been trying to get somewhere, but all I do is ride around the block looking for something to be. But the truth is I'm not going anywhere, I'm just going there fast. You see, I'm a cab and cab's don't go to places they want to go. They go where other people tell them. And when there's nobody to tell them where to go, they don't know what to do, so they just ride around the block forever.

A distant melody.

If I could only hear that voice inside me once in a while, that song.

The melody fades again.

The stars come out.

To be what I am, what I really am is not as easy as all that. Because I could be a million things. Sometimes I feel like a space traveller, looking for my star. How many millions and billions of infinities are there?

DEWEY

That's Orion. See?

CAB

I'd like to be an astronomer. Discover the unknown.

DEWEY

Are you interested in astronomy?

CAB

Not really.

DEWEY

Oh.

CAB

But what difference does that make? My father's a dentist.
You think he's interested in teeth?

DEWEY

I want to be an astronaut. I want to go right there. That's
where I come from. That's where my people are now. Did
you know that, Cab?

CAB

No, I didn't.

DEWEY

They left me here many years ago with that woman who
calls herself my mother and now they're waiting for me to
return.

CAB

So why don't you be an astronaut, Dewey? Astronaut is a
career anyway.

DEWEY

For one thing, they don't take a lot of women in the space program.

CAB

Oh, right. I forgot. You're a woman.

DEWEY

So there's *that* biological drawback.

CAB

You shouldn't think of it as a drawback, Dewey. Some people are women and some people are men. And then there's the school librarian.

DEWEY

You've always thought of me as just one of the guys, right?

CAB

Yeah. Well, not a "guy," Dewey. A friend, yeah.

DEWEY

I mean, since we were kids it hasn't made any difference to you has it.

CAB

Not really, no.

DEWEY

So how come, all of a sudden, there's this big thing happening?

CAB

What thing?

DEWEY

I don't know. People at school are saying "Hey, are you two going out?"

CAB

Who? Me and you?

DEWEY

Yes.

CAB

That's unbelievable. She's my best friend. We've hung around for years and nobody's said anything. Naturally, my parents wouldn't interfere in something like that. In fact, I'm not sure they even know what sex Dewey is. As a matter of fact, I'm not sure they even know what sex *I* am.

MOM

You're male. I know that.

DAD

And she's female. *(A look from CAB)* Isn't she?

MOM

And that's okay.

CAB

It's not okay. But people at school think we're going out.

MOM

Well, she is a woman and you're a man, and that sort of thing happens. Sometimes.

CAB

A man? I don't think of myself as a man when I'm around Dewey, and I don't think of her as a woman. I always just thought of us as buddies. Until now.

MOM

Well, I think that's a very positive, non-sexist attitude to have.

CAB

A lot you know, Mom. The unfortunate truth is that people at school aren't very positive or non-sexist. In fact, they're exactly the opposite.

DAD

Do you have to be like them?

CAB

(Yes.)

DAD

What?

CAB

Look, I know you people raised me in a kind of liberal atmosphere. Not to see any difference between men and women, but there *are* differences.

MOM

Biological differences.

CAB

Well, I don't know about you, folks, but that's pretty important at my age. And I just don't want people to think I'm going out with someone when I'm not. Especially someone who's sort of like one of the *guys*, you know?

DAD

What do you care what people think? People everywhere are like sheep. They follow the fold. But you're not like that.

CAB

Oh, right. I forgot. (Baa)

MOM

We brought you up to be yourself. Not what others want you to be.

CAB

But I *am* what others want me to be. That's my whole identity. I didn't have the heart to tell them, naturally. Not after they went to so much trouble and anguish bringing me up in completely the opposite way. Instead, Dewey and I have quietly agreed not to hang out for a while. We're still friends and everything, but the problem is that I'm beginning to develop a kind of obsession all of a sudden. I'm starting to imagine what she'd look like in a dress. My best friend. I've had other thoughts as well, that I won't go into at this point. But I've even started to dream about her, recently. It's kind of sexual. Is that normal?

DAD

Normal? What's normal?

CAB

Thanks, Dad. Not you — that's for sure. *(Off on his own)*

Passing DEWEY *in the hall at school.*

CAB

Oh. Hi.

DEWEY

Hi.

SONG.

• 3 •

CAB

I went to the counsellor, for some career counselling the other day. I decided I wanted to be a career counsellor. I got out all the books. But I never read them. I know everything there is to know about careers anyway. You see, I thought about being them all. I'm trying to build myself from the ground up, but at the moment, construction is at a standstill here. I've investigated every walk of life and now I stand at the crossroads, unable to go anywhere because frankly I could either go in every direction at once, or in no direction at all — which seems to be where I'm heading at the moment.

DEEK

You could be fat and stupid.

CAB

Fat and stupid is not a career, Deek. Unless you're the vice principal.

DEEK

No. But it's a lifestyle.

CAB

(Suddenly) That's what I need! That's it! I need a lifestyle! A whole thing to go along with my personality.

DEEK

What personality? I thought you didn't have one.

CAB

My lifestyle will *define* me. Think about somebody with a really greedy lifestyle, for example.

DEEK

My Dad.

CAB

I was speaking rhetorically. But alright. Your Dad. What does your Dad do for a living? Investment portfolios, right?

DEEK

I guess. Who cares, man.

CAB

He found a life that suits his greed. It's perfect. Everything he is. His clothes, his house, his job, his incredibly unhappy, but greedy little child, are a product of his greedy lifestyle. He doesn't have to even think about what he wants anymore. He knows. "What would you like, sir?" Why the greediest thing there is, of course. "That would be the thirty-six-ounce serving of raw meat, sir." "Perfect. I'll have two."

DEEK

Well, he really likes his steak rare, that's for sure.

CAB

Of course he does. It's him. But me. What am I? Tell me what I am, Deek, before I disappear off the face of the earth. What do I seem like to you?

DEEK

A guy, I guess.

CAB

I wonder if you could be a bit more specific.

DEEK

I don't know. You're sort of smart.

CAB

Smart? Do you think I'm smart? Really?

DEEK

Smarter than me.

CAB

Okay. So I'm smarter than dried concrete. What else?

DEEK

Well, you sure like to bullshit a lot.

CAB

Yes. I could be an English teacher.

DEEK

You always tell people what they want to hear.

CAB

I do, don't I?

DEEK

Like you're really quite a brown-noser is what I mean,
Cab. A big, giant suckhole.

CAB

You have such an artful way with words, Deek. But you
also have a point. I have a flare for saying whatever is
popular, whether I believe it or not. I really ought to go
into politics.

DEEK

Why don't you run for president, then?

CAB

Of the school? Hm. I suppose school president is a start —
however pathetic. I'll do it. And you'll run with me, Deek,
as my incredibly incompetent vice president.

                              DEEK

Me?

                               CAB

We'll do exactly like the real guys.

                              DEEK

Vice president?

                               CAB

(Wandering off) Let's see now. What promises can we
make that can't possibly be kept?

   SONG.

   Preparation for the campaign.

                             • 4 •

                               CAB

Fellow students, I just want to say a *few* words, because I
think that the candidates should be brief and to the point.
After all, the truth is simple.

                               MOM

You don't have to run for school president. We're not
pressuring you.

                               CAB

I know. Don't remind me.

                               42

                              DAD

Whatever you want.

                              CAB

Whatever you want. That's what people should be
promising in this campaign. Because that's what you
deserve. After all — who is this school for? Teachers?
Teachers — and let me say that I admire the work that
they do here — are but facilitators for our education. It is
for our benefit that this school exists in the first place. We
should have more of a say in how it operates. We should
be running the life of our school, the school should not be
running — the life — of — what am I trying to say here,
Deek. That we should run the school, the school should
not run us. That's it.

                             DEEK

It's great, man. I'd vote for you.

                              CAB

You *are* going to vote for me.

                             DEEK

Right. Right on.

                              CAB

You really think it's good?

                             DEEK

People are digging your message a lot.

                               43

CAB

It's a good message, even if I do say so myself. "We should be running the school."

DEEK

Yeah. Power to the people. It's like a revolution around here. You've inspired a lot a folks, man.

CAB

Inspired? That wasn't my intention. But I didn't have the heart to say it. So I just went along with everybody else. Baa. And as I spoke to them about freedom and change and self-determination, I felt pulled along by my own words. I was, for a moment anyway, who I pretended to be. I couldn't seem to get off the wave that I'd created. The wave that swept me into power. Yeah, I thought. I'm going to start making changes around here! I'm going to be the people's president, man! Yeah!

DEWEY

Well, you'd better do something, then.

CAB

(Abrupt change of tone) Do? What can I do? I can't possibly make good on this.

DEWEY

Then resign with dignity and go into seclusion.

CAB

That would be too humiliating. Who's ever resigned from politics before they were even caught?

DEWEY

Then you're going to have to find a way to make it all happen.

CAB

What? Students running the school? You've got to be kidding. What teacher in his right mind trusts a student as far as he can throw him.

DEWEY

Some of the teachers actually agree with you. Sort of. People believe in you, Cab.

CAB

Why do people choose to believe in other people in the first place?

DEWEY

Because the people they believe in have the plan. They believe in you, and then they crucify you. Just ask Jesus.

CAB

Plan? Me? Dewey — I get lost in washrooms. You know me. Where am I going to lead anybody? Except down the toilet?

DEWEY

You're the president now.

CAB

Yeah. Great.

DEWEY
Congratulations. *(She gives him a kiss.)*

CAB
Oh.

*An awkward pause as they both try to recover
from the kiss which was really nothing much.*

So why are you wearing that outfit?

DEWEY
This? I don't know.

CAB
What's wrong? What did I say? I'm sorry.

DEWEY
It's okay. I look ridiculous. I know.

CAB
No. Just — different than usual.

DEWEY
I suppose I should have gotten into this whole scene
earlier in life? But how did I know?

CAB
What scene would that be?

DEWEY
Being a woman, Cab.

CAB

Most women don't look anything like this, I hate to tell you.

DEWEY

It's a statement about the way I feel.

CAB

Pretty bad, then?

DEWEY

I feel so unhappy, Cab. I hate this. I just don't fit in here. I hate the whole thing. I think I'm going to leave school and go somewhere.

CAB

You are? No. Don't leave school. I'm the president. I'll change everything.

DEWEY

You can't change the way people think. I'm a freak to them.

CAB

So just look normal, and nobody will pay any attention to you.

DEWEY

But I wouldn't *feel* normal, Cab!

CAB

Will you stay, Dewey? Please?

                              DEWEY
Why should I?

                               CAB
For me?

                              DEWEY
You? You don't even care about me anymore. You've got a
whole bunch of glamourous new friends.

                               CAB
Not like you. I don't have anybody to talk to. I miss
talking to you.

                              DEWEY
Well . . . I miss you too.

                               CAB
I mean, you're like my friend. My best friend.

            *They give each other a friendly punch on the
            arm.*

                               CAB
I only hang around with those guys for the sake of
appearances, Dewey. I want you to know that.

                              DEWEY
I suppose that's some consolation.

                               CAB
I'm so confused about my feelings for her. I don't know
what I'm thinking half the time. I can't hear this song. This

                                48

song. What is it singing to me? Something. Why don't I know my own feelings? Probably because I haven't got any. I've been driving other people around for so long, like some passenger in the back. So passenger, tell me where to go now. Dewey's such a strange girl. Is it any wonder I have such strange feelings about her? She's right about one thing. She is a freak. And I don't mind, but everybody at school knows it. Poor Dewey. She's started showing up, wearing women's clothes and makeup, but not the way any ordinary girl might, so that she'd just fade away, like so many people do around here, but as a *statement*. I think that even if she *had* tried just to be ordinary, she couldn't. She can't hide what she is. She'll always be Dewey. And me? Well, I have my image.

                          DEWEY
So — I'll see you later?

                           CAB
Yeah. Okay. Uh...around the back?

                          DEWEY
(Resigned) Sure.

        SONG.

        CAB *sprays graffiti on the banner, disappears.*

DEEK

(Bringing ladder to remove banner) So far, you're the worst president this school has ever had.

CAB

I know.

DEEK

People are really disappointed in you.

CAB

You don't need to rub it in.

DEEK

Everybody thought there were going to be some big changes around here. You don't even show up to council meetings half the time.

CAB

When did you develop this political consciousness, Deek? Did I miss something?

DEEK

I'm vice president, remember? If anything happens to you, I take over as president, you know. Even if you're booted out of office.

CAB

It's just a game. People playing at politics. Man. And what

"changes" does everybody expect, exactly? The world doesn't work that way.

CAB

DEEK

We want to be masters of our own destiny, Cab.

CAB

What?

DEEK

We want to call the shots. We want an end to the oppression!

CAB

What oppression? No street shoes in the gym?

DEEK

I don't know. But that's what you said in one of your speeches. Remember?

CAB

Calling Dr. Frankenstein. Doctor Frankenstein, you've created a monster. Deek. My young friend. *(An arm around him)* My dear companion.

DEEK

Hey. Watch it.

CAB

Sorry. You don't need to remember my speeches. You only need to remember why I made them. So that I could be president. That's all. So that I could win the big popularity contest. And I won. Voilà. The rest is words. If any oppression exists around here, it already exists in the real world. All the racism, the sexism, the stupidity, and might I say the "homophobia," are already out there. This is just a school. If you want to change the world, first, fine.

DEEK

We can start here.

CAB

Alright. I'll pass a decree. And you can stand on a table in the cafeteria and delivery it. Just like in a revolution.

DEEK

You've become so cynical, man.

CAB

I've always *been* cynical. This should come as no surprise to you. Or to anybody. Why all the disappointment?

DEEK

Because I believed in you. In what you were.

CAB

What I was? I'm nothing. This is Cab you're talking to here. Hop in and tell me where you want to go and how you want to get there.

DEEK

And why don't you hang around with Dewey anymore?

CAB

Dewey? I associate with Dewey regularly.

DEEK

She told me about your secret meetings. What are you afraid of? That some of the fabulous people you hang with won't approve?

CAB

The people I "hang" with are indeed quite fabulous, and fairly sophisticated, and frankly no they wouldn't. Dewey's a bit too much of an individual for them, I'm afraid.

DEEK

What's happening to you? Cheerleaders and jocks, man? It's like a TV sit-com. With you in the lead role.

CAB

Yes. But I *am* in the lead role.

Song.

CAB in spotlight.

• 6 •

CAB

Deek is right, of course. I am becoming a complete asshole. But at least I'm becoming *something*. Up to this point I haven't been sure what I was, and now it's being defined for me. Just like I predicted, once I find a lifestyle — in this case the asshole lifestyle — I begin to make easy choices around it. I suck up to all the right people and ignore the wrong ones. Wrong being defined as anybody who isn't right.

MOM
Only life isn't quite so black and white as that, Cab.

CAB
But it's what I am now, Mom. I'm just being myself.

MOM
Well, that's fine then.

CAB
I could be a lot worse.

MOM
If you like.

CAB
How far could I get to, I wonder, before my parents would finally say "Stop! This is as far as we want to go. Whoa! Let us out!" I think probably quite a distance.

MOM
We're not going to interfere. Are we, Dad?

DAD
Just be true to yourself. Whatever you do.

CAB

Myself? That's a good one. Where's that guy, I wonder. Sometimes in class, I write my name over and over again, as if by some magic, the letters might re-form themselves into a word, just a single word of information about me. When I *am* in class, that is. I've become rather addicted to missing school and hanging out in the mall of late. Wait. Here's me. I found myself after all. *(Joined by* DEWEY *as he speaks)* Here I am, leaning up against the wall of the video arcade. The school president.

DEWEY

This isn't you, Cab.

CAB

Then who are you talking to? Who says it isn't?

DEWEY

Maybe it's the person you think you are now, but it's not the person I remember.

CAB

How touching. Tell me about him.

DEWEY

Just this guy. I'll show you. *(With a photobooth photo)* Here he is. Having his photo taken with an old buddy of his. See? Recognize him, Cab? Neither do I, 'cause he's alive and you're dead. And this place is your tomb, man. Some empty mall for you empty dreams. This crypt. This place that buries you in sad merchandise and consumes your soul.

CAB

That's real poetry, Dewey. That's beautiful.

DEWEY

It's only the truth.

CAB

What soul? You misunderstood my nature. You just didn't know what I was really like. That's all. And now you do. What are you looking at?

DEWEY

I'm just trying to see through all that.

CAB

I've got to go.

DEWEY

Sure.

CAB

I don't know where. But I've got to go.

DEWEY

Cab?

CAB

What?

DEWEY

What's the difference between truth and lies?

CAB

I don't know. What's the difference between truth and lies?

DEWEY

You really don't know, do you?

CAB

Is that a joke?

DEWEY

I wish it was.

CAB

(*Sudden shift*) So Dewey's become profound all of a sudden. Deep long looks and heavy sighs. Me? I'm becoming more and more shallow to make up for it.

CAROLINE

Really?

CAB

Yeah.

CAROLINE

That's cool.

CAB

Why is it cool?

CAROLINE

I don't know. You ask such weird questions all the time.

CAB

Do I?

CAROLINE

See?

CAB

What's weird about that?

CAROLINE

I don't know.

CAB

And she really doesn't know. Caroline doesn't know anything. I guess that's why I've decided to go out with her for a while. Or is it she who's decided to go out with me? Never mind. As much of a jerk as I am, Caroline is the least likely to find out about it, and even if she did, the least likely to care. Caroline is the shallowest person, next to me, that I've ever known. Why do you go out with me, Caroline?

CAROLINE

Because you're the president of the school this year, Cab. And every year I go out with whoever's president. It's a tradition with me. Ever since grade nine.

CAB

So that's it. I knew there was a feeling of predestiny about the whole thing. So what do you think, Dad?

DAD

She seems nice.

58

CAB

She's not.

DAD

Oh, well . . .

CAB

Whatever I want. I know.

DAD

Whatever.

CAB

The thing is, I don't want Caroline at all. But then, Caroline doesn't really want me either. I'm just part of her history. Already. So the whole thing works out rather well. Two people looking shallowly into one another's eyes. Did you say every year, whoever's president?

CAROLINE

Whoever.

CAB

What happens if the president is a female?

CAROLINE

A what? Oh.

CAB

It's interesting how we so seldom think of women in positions of power. It would never have a occurred to Caroline that the president would be another woman, because it goes against her traditional view of the world,

59

and her place in it. Fortunately, for Caroline, the unthinkable has never happened in this school. And this is her last year. But raising the question alone seems to have shattered a major preconception in her mind. As if she's always believed the world was flat or something. She hasn't been the same since then. Her shallowness has become a kind of poetic frailty now.

                    CAROLINE
Look. I'm reading this now.

                    CAB
What is it?

                    CAROLINE
I don't know. But the cover looks really sad.

                    CAB
Oh, yes. It does.

        SONG.

                    • 7 •

                    CAB
I've decided I'll try being politically correct for a little while. I mean, I am president, and quickly losing popularity. I've gotten into a whole ecology thing. I'm even dressing the part, trading in my political look for something more "whole earth." I've started a campaign called "Let's go environ - mental." Instituted recycling in a big way. People have volunteered as watchdogs.

He tosses away a wrapper.

> DEEK

Hey! Pick that up!

> CAB

Actually, I think I meant it as kind of a joke. A sort of comment on how crazy people can go with this kind of stuff. And sure enough. Everybody's gone crazy.

> DEEK

What are we doing with plastic?

> CAB

I don't know. I couldn't care less about the environment.

> DEEK

It's our future, man.

> CAB

Maybe it's your future, Deek, but I need to sort out my own garbage before I start sorting out other people's.

> DEEK

It happens to be your responsibility.

> CAB

No it isn't. *(Tossing down the same wrapper he just picked up)* It's yours.

> DEEK

Pick that up!

CAB

Pick it up yourself, if you're so concerned.

DEEK

Wow, Cab. You're nuts.

CAB

Perhaps I'm going "environ - mental."

DEEK

You don't even believe in your own program!

CAB

This isn't my program, Deek. This is the popular program. Personally, I haven't got a program.

DEEK

You better get one.

CAB

He's right, of course. But naturally I don't have the heart to tell him. Anyway, what would I tell him? How can I admit to not even existing? How can I tell him I'm the invisible man. This morning I woke up and I wasn't even there anymore There was some guy I didn't recognize, but I was nowhere to be found. So I'm on the lookout for where I might have gone. Let's see. Where did I go? Whoa! There I am! In the park, sitting up against a tree, stoned out of my head, dreaming about another life. The one I don't have.

STONED VOICE IN THE SHADOWS

Try this, if you think that's cool.

CAB

I don't really have the heart to say no. Life is too complicated. Too unclear. I'm just trying to hear that voice. So I just say yes. And what happens after that is hard to say.

MOM

You don't remember.

CAB

Actually, I forget whether I remember or not.

MOM

Well, I'll tell you, then. They brought you home in a police car.

CAB

So the police found me. I should have thought of those guys. I was looking for myself, I should have called them first, and told them how lost I was.

DAD

What are you talking about?

CAB

Do you even care?

DAD

Of course we care.

MOM

We don't want you taking drugs.

                              CAB
So try and stop me, then.

                              MOM
We're not going to stop you.

                              DAD
We're going to let you do whatever you want. We always
have.

                              CAB
What if I die?

                              MOM
You won't die.

                              CAB
How do you know?

                              DAD
We have faith in you.

                              CAB
Faith? In me? No. Don't have faith in me. I'm not Santa
Claus. What am I? Nothing.

                              DAD
Our son.

                              CAB
But it's so vague, folks. I didn't get a manual with this
model. Maybe you could give me a clue what you want

here. But they don't say anything. They never do. I live with two, smiling, nodding heads.

DEWEY

I live with only one head and she never smiles. She's a dead person from the dead planet. I think she's made of wax. I pinched her. I said "You're just a mechanical mother from motherland. I recognize your moving parts from Disneyworld." She pinched me back. That surprised me. I said "Wow, mother." She said "You're weird." I said "Excuse me Bride of Frankenstein. . . . *I'm* weird? I know you ate my father!" That shut her up.

CAB

Is that lipstick, Dewey?

DEWEY

It's a statement about lipstick.

CAB

I don't have the heart to tell her she looks a little odd like that. Anyway she knows. It's not like everybody isn't already letting her know. In the subtle way people let you know things around here. And if that's what she wants to be — wants to be? I sound like them now. That's what I am! I'm them! Of course! I'm becoming my parents. Slowly but surely the tell-tale signs are creeping up on me. My father became a dentist because he didn't know he wanted to be a violinist. My mother didn't know she wanted to become a clown, so she married one instead. So that's it! The truth comes too late in life. You find out what you are, but not until you're already something else. No wonder I've started doing drugs.

65

SONG.

Acid inkglob effect.

Silhouette dancing.

• 8 •

CAB

When it comes right down to it, drugs isn't really me. But then, what is? I hoped that perhaps I would hear my own voice singing. But I haven't heard anything yet. And while most people's parents are really on their case about drugs, mine don't seem to take any notice at all. I know they're just pretending not to notice anything. I leave all sorts of paraphernalia around, just to make it look like I'm doing more than I am. But they walk right through it all. I think it's some kind of reverse psychology.

DEEK

My Dad's idea of reverse psychology is to hit me on the head.

CAB

That's not reverse psychology, Deek.

DEEK

He does it with the back of his hand.

CAB

Poor Deek. What a life. But at least his Dad notices him. Even if he doesn't like what he sees. At least Deek is a child in his parent's eye. Mine try to treat me like an adult all the time, discussing things with me that, frankly, I don't think parents should discuss with their children.

MOM

Such as what?

CAB

Well, I can't say it, can I? Because that would be discussing it.

MOM

You mean sex.

CAB

I mean a lot of things.

MOM

Now I know you mean sex, because whenever you say "a lot of things," you mean sex.

CAB

You think you know me so well. They think I'm going to sit down with them, maybe over a glass of wine in the evening, and discuss my sex life with them.

MOM

So you do mean sex.

CAB

Frankly, it's embarrassing. And anyway, what do they know? It's not that I need to know how to have sex. I've read everything there is to know about that. It's everything else leading up to that point. I mean, I'm the guy who doesn't know what he wants, right? I can't even decide on a flavour of ice cream.

DEWEY

I thought you *had* a girlfriend.

CAB

She chose *me*. Caroline likes me for who I am, not what I am. She goes out with the president, Dewey. Not whoever it happens to be.

DEWEY

Isn't that incredibly shallow.

CAB

Yeah. So we're really the perfect match.

DEWEY

I don't think you're shallow, Cab.

CAB

The truth is, I don't think I even like women, Dewey.

DEWEY

Really?

CAB

I don't think so.

DEWEY

Do you like guys?

CAB

Gee. I don't think so. Maybe I do. Wouldn't that be a kick.

DEWEY

Yeah.

CAB

What's wrong?

DEWEY

No. That's cool. I guess.

She shrugs, and wanders off.

CAB

(Calling after her) So are you disappointed? My God. I think I wanted her to say she was. Can that be? Oh, voice. Voice. Sing something to me. Tell me how I feel. Because I think I know what I want for once. Just a little tiny feeling right here. Dewey. Could it be? She is a woman. Yes. But it's not really the woman part of her that I like. It's the Dewey part. Maybe that's what I am. I'm not a heterosexual or a homosexual, I'm a Deweysexual. There's a new idea. Your sexuality defined by the person you actually like instead of the other way around. Whoa! I think these drugs are starting to get to me. I nearly convinced myself of something there. Dewey? Whoa!

69

                              DEEK
So why don't you stop. You've said a million times how
you hate the way drugs make you feel. How depressed
you always are.

                              CAB
Yes. But there are appearances to keep up.

                              DEEK
Is that all you do anything for anymore? Appearances?

                              CAB
I never noticed but you're sort of attractive, you know,
Deek, in a fat, stupid sort of way.

                              DEEK
What?

                              CAB
Would it bother you if I gave you a little kiss on the cheek?
Right here?

                              DEEK
Yes!

                              CAB
Why? Appearances, Deek? Is that all you do anything for
anymore?

                              DEEK
You're evil, man.

That's what I am! I'm evil!

Song.

He dresses in "odd" clothes.

•9•

CAB

Did I mention that I've given up drugs for a while so that I can concentrate being evil, full time?

CAROLINE

Deek says you're gay. The word's spreading.

CAB

Oh, that's right. I forgot to tell you.

CAROLINE

What?

CAB

Well, I didn't imagine it would interfere with your plans. I'm still president, after all.

CAROLINE

I heard they're trying to get rid of you. I heard you're never at council meetings.

CAB

That's because I'm studying to be evil. Right now I'm preparing for the L.S.A.T.

CAROLINE

You're going into law?

CAB

I'm going to defend corporate criminals. But only the guilty ones. I plan on making lots of money.

CAROLINE

That's pretty unprincipled, Cab. How much money?

CAB

Inquiring minds want to know. I guess my sexuality isn't a problem for you then.

CAROLINE

You're just going around saying you're gay to get attention.

CAB

Am I?

CAROLINE

You do everything to get attention, Cab.

CAB

For a shallow person, that's pretty perceptive.

CAROLINE

That's the consensus of the psychology class anyway.

CAB

You discuss my personality in psychology?

CAROLINE

We discuss whoever doesn't show up. It's a way of keeping attendance really high. We discuss you a lot.

CAB

I don't believe this. Now I'm going to have to start attending classes at this school.

CAROLINE

We think you don't get enough love at home. We think you take drugs because your parents don't care enough about you.

CAB

My parents just let me do whatever I want.

CAROLINE

And we think that's wrong.

CAB

Why don't you people discuss your own problems?

CAROLINE

(Going) The truth hurts, doesn't it?

CAB

Attention? I don't want attention! I just want someone to notice me, before I fade away and disappear. This is humiliating, people sitting around discussing me as if I was a class project. What am I? Something sitting in formaldehyde, waiting to be dissected by those — those — amateurs. Even professional psychologists can't figure me out, and I've always prided myself on that. And now — I'm reduced to nothing more than an assignment. Attention? Four-year-olds want attention. I want applause!

MOM

Maybe you should go into the theatre.

CAB

Thanks, Mom. I'll tell you when I need your . . . did you just give me advice? Was that a suggestion I actually heard you utter?

MOM

I'm only pointing out one of many alternatives. You can choose it if you want.

CAB

If I want. Yeah. I know. I know.

MOM

But it seems to me if you crave so much attention all the time, and you claim to be a million different people, all in one, you can turn that into something.

CAB

The theatre. I could be *really* evil on stage. Without going to all the trouble. Think how evil I could be.

MOM

Of course you could. You could be anything.

CAB

Just like life. Only I could be them all. I could be a drug addict without actually having to do drugs. I could be a president, without any of the responsibility. I could be gay without being so...misunderstood. I could be a clown, or a violinist, or an astronomer. I could be an architect, and build my own world to live in! I could be everything I want to be for just a little bit, and then walk off the stage and forget about it. The theatre! It's a brilliant idea! But I don't have the heart to tell her so I won't. I'll just pretend to be ungrateful as usual. She'll understand.

SONG.

CAB *rehearses being himself.*

• 10 •

CAB *meets* DEEK *who's with* CAROLINE.

CAB

No. Let me guess. I've been booted out of office and you've been made president, Deek. Am I right?

                         DEEK
How did you know?

                         CAB
Hello Caroline.

                         DEEK
I can explain.

                         CAB
No you can't.

                         DEEK
No, I can't.

                         CAB
Only Caroline could ever explain.

                         DEEK
I was hoping you wouldn't be too pissed off, Cab. I mean
— taking over as president and then taking over —
well . . .

                         CAB
They were just roles I was playing, Deek. And now you're
playing them.

                         DEEK
So you're not angry?

                         CAB
Well, you have mentioned to many people around here

that I'm a homosexual. Which is quite incorrect, as a matter of fact.

DEEK

Oh, that. Yeah. Well, sorry.

CAB

And it has sort of ruined my life here, because you know how incredibly unsophisticated people can be around here. Especially about that. And it pretty well destroys my chances of going out with other girls now because they'll all think I have AIDS I suppose, because of how totally misinformed people are on that issue. And so basically I'm damaged for the rest of my life, because when we all look back fondly on our years here, as I'm sure we all will, I'll have nothing to look back on but fear and loathing, and a friend who stabbed me in the back. But no — I'm not angry, Deek. Because I intend to get even.

DEEK

I don't like the way you say that.

CAB

Neither do I. I've devised a suitable revenge for both of you. I'm putting you in my play.

DEEK

What play?

CAB

Didn't I tell you. Owing to my sudden interest in the theatre, and the fact that I happen to know that the drama teacher is an alcoholic who cheats on his wife regularly,

I've been given permission to stage a small production of the story of my life. All the characters from my life will be in it, saying and doing all the wonderful things they do. I, of course, will be portraying me. You two will be played by other actors.

DEEK

What drug are you on now?

CAROLINE

I'm good at theatre. I could be myself.

CAB

Caroline, you couldn't be yourself if you tried. None of us could. We can only pretend to be.

DEEK

Not everyone is a phony, Cab.

CAB

What are we, Deek? Are we real people? *(Shoving him)* Is this real?

DEEK

Watch it.

CAB

This is all make-believe, folks. We're just acting out a part and those of us who haven't got a part yet are looking for one to act. Right now, Deek is acting cool.

DEEK

Do you want me to hit you, Cab? Right here?

CAROLINE

That's what he wants according to psychology class. It'll
prove that you have feelings for him.

CAB

Feelings? For a guy? That would be too much for Deek.
He'd rather have no feelings at all. He'd rather be a dead
person, than who he is. The guy is so petrified of his own
sexuality that he goes around spreading rumours about
other people's, just to throw them off the scent. Isn't that
right, Deek? Maybe you should discuss him in your
psychology class, Caroline. A classic case of sexual
insecurity. Do you even like Caroline, Deek? Or is this just
a cover for what you really are?

DEEK

I swear, Cab.

CAB

Hey. It doesn't matter if you hit me or not. It's all fake
anyway. The whole rotten show. And you know it!

DEEK punches CAB.

CAB

Oof!

DEEK

Is that real enough for you?

DEEK storms off.

                    CAROLINE
If it's any consolation, I wish you were still president, Cab.
I liked you a lot better than him.

        She goes.

                    CAB
Well, that is a consolation, but I don't have the heart to tell
her. As for Deek, I think he'll make a perfect president.
He's too stupid to listen to anybody, so he'll have to
actually think for himself. As for me — I've got this play
to put on.

                    DEWEY
And there's a kissing scene?

                    CAB
But it's with me. It'll be like, you know, nothing.

                    DEWEY
And in front of everybody.

                    CAB
Everybody who shows up. That could be nobody.

                    DEWEY
But how does it fit in with the plot? I don't get it.

                    CAB
They fall in love. Sort of.

DEWEY

That's kind of sappy, isn't it, Cab? Knowing you.

CAB

Well. It's a joke. You know. Like, the "happy ending."
Don't you like it?

DEWEY

Yeah. It's really funny.

Suddenly, she runs off.

CAB

So what's *her* problem?

SONG.

Two monks appear with candles.

*CAB, in the middle, kneels, as the monks
disappear.*

• 11 •

CAB

I have a voice that tells me things. It sings me songs and
sometimes I listen but mostly the noise in my head is far
too loud to hear the melody that's going on up here. It's
like all the channels are on at once. There's definitely
something wrong with my antenna. But someday I'll get it
tuned to myself. And then I'll know what I am. So I've

taken up meditation. Welcome to the spiritual section of my life. I've decided to be a monk.

DEWEY

Yeah? What happened to the play?

CAB

What else *could* happen? It was the story of my life so nobody knew what it was about. And everybody quit. Of course. You were only the first of many.

DEWEY

Sorry I ran out on you. I couldn't take the pressure.

CAB

What? Are you kidding? I'm very philosophical about it now. Trying to be anyway. After all, it was just one phase of me, like the many phases of the moon.

DEWEY

Obviously you're still doing dope.

CAB

For spiritual reasons only. I'm developing my consciousness, you see. I'm trying to get in touch with the inner self. Meditation is a real high. But occasionally, I need to get a little higher.

DEWEY

I'm going to a shrink now.

CAB

For some reason I loathe conventional psychology.

DEWEY

She says the unhappiness is only temporary. But I feel more permanent about it somehow. Like a trip up and down an endless flight of stairs.

CAB

It only about seventy more years, Dewey. Then it's over. Anyway — I never thought of *you* as unhappy.

DEWEY

I never knew you thought of me at all.

CAB

Of course I do. I love you, Dewey. *(Pause)* I love everybody now.

DEWEY

Oh. Well, that's good. So you're not evil anymore?

CAB

I don't plan on going into corporate law, if that's what you mean. No. I think I'll be a dentist like my Dad. It's a sort of Zen-like, nothing kind of career.

DEWEY

But it's not you, Cab.

                            CAB

(Suddenly emotional) How do you know what's me? Huh?
How come everybody knows what's me except me?

                            DEWEY

I know what *isn't* you.

                            CAB

I'm just looking for something to be, Dewey. We're all just
looking for something to be. Somewhere to go —
something to do — and maybe someone to do it with.
That's all we're looking for. That's all we ask in life. But
what do we get? Choices. But choices that turn out to be
no choice at all, really. Because we are what we are and
that's the end of it. Wherever we come from, that's where
we end up, no matter how far we go in the opposite
direction. We can't run away from that. We can only
become what we were meant to be all along. In my case,
that's not much of anything. Not a great leader, or thinker,
or anything. Just this. You want to know why my parents
never care about any of the things I do. Because they know
I can't escape what I am. Which is incredibly, painfully
ordinary. I'm nothing. That's what I am now, and that's
what I always was. And that's what I'm destined to
become.

                            DEWEY

You're not nothing to *me*, Cab.

                            CAB

No?

                             84

DEWEY

No.

CAB

What am I, then? To *you*.

DEWEY

A fucked-up human being. Just like the rest of us.

CAB

Thankyou.

DEWEY

Besides that? Let's see. You're selfish. Thoughtless.
Conceited. Would you like me to go on?

CAB

Not really, Dewey. This is my life, thanks. Just stay out of
it.

DEWEY

No. It's my life. While you've been going through all this
. . . stuff, so have I. But I guess you just didn't notice.
'Cause I guess you just don't see me, Cab. Like I'm out in
the universe here. Just like you. See? And I'm not *nothing*,
man! Maybe I'm floating around in the dark, but I'm
something. I exist. Do you see me, Cab? 'Cause if you
don't see anything except yourself, then you'll always be
alone. I don't want to be alone, Cab. I want to be a part of
the world. What do you want?

CAB

I want . . . *(Pause)*

DEWEY

When you figure it out, let me know.

DEWEY goes, leaving him.

SONG.

• 11 (a) •

DEWEY

The thing is, sir — ma'am, well, it's my opinion that your son needs to get out a little more and enjoy life.

MOM

He has been up in his room a lot, yes.

DAD

Doing God only knows what.

DEWEY

So the thing is, you see, I've come to ask permission to take him to the prom, if that's okay.

DAD

Whatever.

MOM

It's up to you.

DEWEY

Oh. Good. I'm glad you folks don't find that too weird or anything.

DAD

Weird? What's weird?

MOM

We've come to expect the unexpected around here.

DAD

Cab's a pretty unpredictable guy.

DEWEY

Well...the truth is, I think your son is a little confused about himself at the moment.

DAD

That's okay.

MOM

Aren't we all.

DEWEY

Wow. You really are what he says you are.

MOM

We are?

DEWEY

Just two, smiling, nodding heads, man. It's no wonder.

                            DAD
What else should we be?

                          DEWEY
How about parents.

                            DAD
In what sense, Dewey?

                          DEWEY
Parents? I don't know.

                            MOM
Does anyone, really?

                          DEWEY
Huh?

                            MOM
All we can be is ourselves. The rest is up to him.

                            DAD
We haven't the vaguest idea how to raise a child.

                            MOM
Never have.

                          DEWEY
You don't?

MOM

Who does?

DEWEY

Wow.

MOM

Someday when you have children of your own — you
won't have any idea either.

DEWEY

I thought parents were supposed to know something
about all this.

MOM

So did we — until we became them.

They smile, as DEWEY *looks on in wonder.*

Music covers the exit.

• 12 •

CAB

My name is Cab. I was created in the image of my mother
and my father, on some rainy night, in the back of a taxi.
Or so the story goes. I was destined for no greatness on the
planet earth — so says a voice inside of me. But I'm here
and this is where I belong. I will live my life on a quiet
street, if that's okay — in some anonymous town; like a

star inside a neighbouring galaxy, just one of the infinite many.

DEEK

Do you really believe that?

CAB

No, but it sounds very humble and gracious, and this is my humble and gracious period.

DEEK

Still, you probably should be honest once in your life, Cab. Especially in a valedictory speech.

CAB

I shouldn't be delivering this anyway. You're the president.

DEEK

Yeah. But I have nothing to say. Anyway, it's the guy with the marks. I can't believe you even passed. You were never here.

CAB

It's where your head is.

DEEK

Still into the spiritual thing?

CAB

I think I'm a little too . . . frivolous for that.

DEEK

Right.

CAB

Hey. No hard feelings, Deek. We both got what we wanted in the end. I hope. You got President, and of course Caroline as your prom date.

DEEK

She really likes me, you know.

CAB

How do you feel about *her*?

DEEK

Okay, I guess. She's pretty.

CAB

Is that the only reason you go out with her?

DEEK

Well, no.

CAB

That's reassuring.

DEEK

Her Dad is president of a big mining company.

CAB

President, eh? You know, Deek — I think the two of you have a great future together.

DEEK

Cab. That stuff you said about me before. You know. Being insecure about my sexuality and that? You haven't said that to anybody else, have you?

CAB

Just a couple of the smaller tabloids.

DEEK

'Cause I'm normal, Cab.

CAB

Normal? Wow. Deek. Don't worry. That secret dies with me. You know what? You're my friend. To me that's *all* you are. The fact that you're normal is never going to change that.

DEEK

(Pause) Thanks.

He goes.

CAB

Poor Deek. Normal. Imagine having to live up to that.

MOM

Imagine having to live up to anything.

CAB

What?

MOM

Except what you are.

CAB

You know, for an old hippie, you're pretty cool, Mom.
Ordinarily I wouldn't have the heart to tell you that,
because I didn't really know where my heart was until
now.

MOM

So who are you taking to the prom?

CAB

I couldn't find a date, so I'm going with Dewey.

MOM

Dewey?

CAB

Well, she belongs to the same species, so I thought what
the hell. Unless you prefer I went with an alien.

MOM

Whatever.

CAB

I don't believe it. But never mind. Nothing about me
surprises my parents anymore. I don't need to see how far
I can go with them. I already know. As far as I possibly
can. And then some. In fact, in certain little ways, my
parents are beginning to surprise *me*. My Mother's signed
up for clown classes. And my Dad's taken up the violin

again. *(Violin)* Unfortunately. If this keeps up, by the time I'm forty, I'll have to move out of the house.

DEWEY

(Eclectically prommed) I should hope so.

CAB

(As stars appear) Well, I'm in no hurry to go anywhere, Dewey. The stars are the same here as anywhere else.

DEWEY

Right.

CAB

I got that job, by the way. In the clothing store. I'm going to enjoy watching other people try different things on for a change, to see if anything fits. What about you? Are you still seeing a shrink?

DEWEY

No. I realized she was just as screwed-up as I am.

CAB

You're not unhappy anymore?

DEWEY

Not at this very moment.

CAB

So we take it moment by moment. Is that it?

                    DEWEY

Something like that.

                    CAB

By the way, that's quite the outfit, Dewey.

                    DEWEY

It's sort of a compromise between my feminine self and
my real self which is yet to be totally defined. What?

                    CAB

Nothing.

                    DEWEY

I thought you said something.

                    CAB

Me. No. I have nothing to say.

                    DEWEY

That's unusual.

                    CAB

I'm an unusual guy.

                    DEWEY

Right. So — do you like it? The outfit?

                    CAB

I like it because you're wearing it. It wouldn't look very
good on me, for example.

DEWEY

(With sounds of the prom dance drifting in) It's such a beautiful night. I almost hate to waste it in there. *(Pause, then answering herself)* Okay. Let's not.

CAB

What? Oh.

There is a long silence.

CAB

I heard a song the other day that I really liked.

DEWEY

Oh, yeah. Where? On the radio?

CAB

No. In my head.

DEWEY

Those are the best kind.

CAB

So would you like to hear it?

DEWEY

I didn't know you were a singer.

CAB

There's a lot of things I'm not. That's never stopped me before.

DEWEY

No.

He sings his little song to her.

DEWEY

That's nice.

CAB

You think maybe I have a career?

DEWEY

I'd keep looking.

CAB

Yeah.

As the SONG plays out, they sit quietly, happily, watching the stars.

The lights fade.

THE END

COST
OF
LIVING

Tim Battle as OUR GUY. *Green Thumb Theatre production.*
Photo by David Cooper.

On video, clumsily recorded, a very boring,
nerdy Social Studies teacher gives out an
assignment — a thousand words on The Cost of
Living. Then, noticing the camera for the first
time, he tells OUR GUY *to turn it off.*

Music.

Pastiche of video images; evocative music. The
pictures are a catalogue of intimate relation-
ships, quarried from magazine advertisements,
and other popular sources. They are familiar to
the audience as being part of the "sex sell" of
everything from beer to nuts. A voice echoes, at
first imperceptible, now overpowering the
music, as OUR GUY *intones:*

I have to have what everybody else has —
I have to be what everybody else is
I have to feel what everybody else feels —
I have to do what everybody else does.
I have to think what everybody else thinks —
I have to . . . I have to. . . .
I have to feel what everybody else does
I have to do what everybody else thinks
I have to want what everybody else has
I have to have what everybody else wants
I have to be what everybody else feels.
I have to . . . I have to . . . have . . . I have to have . . . to
have . . . have to have . . .

Now, with the use of his remote control, he begins a series of short video clips of young people in high school, talking about what they want out of life, now — and in the future.

Every body wants something, don't they sir.

Even you, a mere teacher, want something. Want me . . . want us to *learn* something. Even if I don't *want* it, you *want* it. We all *want* . . . something. In a thousand words or less.

But even education has its price. Yes. Even that. Because there's always the risk that we might actually *learn* something. Yes, everything in life has its cost. It's called the cost of living. You want a thousand-word essay . . . ? That's what you're going to get, sir. Only, I'm going to draw you a picture, because a picture is *worth* a thousand words, so they say. My picture is a portrait . . . a portrait of a guy . . . trying to live . . . in a world . . . where everything has its price . . . and just living can cost you a lot.

Now I wouldn't want to frighten the faint of heart but I've chosen *life* as my main subject, much the way all people tend to choose . . . that . . . as the main subject . . . of living. Stop me if you've heard this.

Remote snaps on couple of quick clips of friends testifying that they are totally preoccupied with sex. Snaps off.

So teacher forgive me if this essay is from my ken and not my pen, from my soul and not my scroll, but somehow I just can't talk about the cost of living without talking about . . . life.

Music, plus clips from various (old and current)
sources concerning sex and young people. He
disappears and reappears with a female man-
nequin; he dances with her for a bit, then
disappears. He returns with a male mannequin,
with whom he dances. He places the male
mannequin next to the female. The song
finished, the clips continue behind him.

Is this what- what- what we aspire to be- be- be- coming?
Dummies? Clothes r- racks? Consumer st- st- st-atistics?
Measurements? Are we just beautiful people . . . with no g-
ge- gen- genit- genita- souls? I ask myself — is that even
close to the truth? I don't know about you, or you, or
especially you — but my experience has been sort of, sort
of the op- op- opposite. My life is totally preoccupied with
se- se- se-my feeling. And why? I wish I knew. God — I
wish I knew. Why can't I think about . . . math . . . he same
way. Why doesn't social stud- stud-studies get me all . . .
hot and ppppassionate.

He thumbs through various current textbooks,
reading passages for their "sexual" content.

There's something about these ideas that turns me on
somewhere in the back of my mind, somewhere at the
back of the class, the image of two . . . atoms . . .
colliding . . . in the middle of the . . . night. That certain
mathematical equation where one figure is placed over
another. Love is — chemistry my friends, physics . . . the
attraction of two opposites . . . bodies in motion . . . only
this experiment is for real. This . . . thing . . . this . . . *life* . . .
is for the practical application of all the text book theories.
That is where it *counts*. Out there where the real Social
Studies is . . . are . . . whatever. And thus begins my class

report on the high cost of living. A living, breathing essay on how I exposed my . . . feelings, at the expense of my cool, to a certain, shall we say, angel, of the female sex, quite strictly speaking. A totally female female by the actual name of Angel. *(He will occasionally use the mannequin to represent her.)* And that is surely what she is. Mostly this essay's for you, Angel. Here I am, you see, embarrassing myself in front of everyone, but it's a small price, and I don't really care. There are greater costs in life, than a bit of embarrassment. It's something I discovered as part of my Social Studies research. My parents, for example paid quite a high price in their time, for their first little act of love. They ended up together. And they ended up with me.

> *TV interview of* MOM *and* DAD'S *love life. It ends with* MOM: "Why are you asking all this. Are you in love? Well, I think that's sweet. I hope you're using condoms."

Their generation, as they tell it, was the age of free love, but as I already pointed out, nothing is really free in this world; there's gotta be a cost for everything; especially making love. And I don't just mean the cost of mouthwash and deodorant, I mean the consequences. After all, we're not just mannequins. We're living, breathing, heaving, sighing biology specimens in Levis. At least we start out in Levis. Who knows where we end up. Who knows where the Levis end up. In the laundry pile of good intentions. Or bad intentions. Or good intentions that turn to bad intentions. I speak, of course, of that fateful night I went to the public library with every intention of researching my essay. In fact, so intent was I on my work that I wasn't really noticing anything around me. At the checkout I hear this voice — "You have an outstanding fine, sir." Huh? I look up, and — speaking of outstanding and fine, there before my very eyes, an older woman. Well, two years older, and as the camera zooms in on me for a close-up, my jaw is like dropped like this and I have become, in a manner of seconds, incapable of even the simplest motor function. How, friends, can I describe true beauty to you? All I know is that when your mouth opens to say "How do you do — I'm so pleased to meet you — what a charming brooch — it goes so well with those sapphire eyes. I'd love to take you out sometime for an evening of wine and scintillating conversation" — it comes out something like "blajjkkkghghg klcnoah." "Excuse me?" she says. I don't know where I got the courage to tell her the truth. "I'm a film director and I'd like to interview you for my documentary." (Right, the documentary of your brain!) "You're a bit young aren't you?" "For what?" "Directing." "Oh, uh . . . it's actually a class project — (what am I saying?) — . . . Social Studies." "Oh" she says, "the study of people. I like that." She says "Well, I guess I'm people — if you think I'd be worth studying." (In minute detail, I'm thinking.)

Fortunately, at this point, you don't know what my mind is doing to you that my body doesn't have the nerve to do. Because even though all I ever think of is sex, I don't want you to think that's all I think. But I can't think of anything else so I don't say anything else, so you just think I'm stupid. I'm not stupid. I just happened to inadvertently stick a pencil through my hand, that's all. "Would you like to meet me after work?" she asks. Hey! I'm supposed to ask that. But all I can do is nod my head like one of those Garfield dolls in the back window of a Honda Civic. *(Nodding)* . . . Yeah . . . Then — she wants me to pay the library fine! This is one classy woman. Very business-like, I'm telling you. Only I don't happen to have the money — so you see, I couldn't take out all those books I intended to, sir. All I managed to check out that night was the librarian. Library assistant, actually.

So now — we cut to the big scene where she meets me after she's finished work. I don't exactly know what's going to happen, but my sweaty armpits seem to. And my hands, and my throat, and my heart and my . . . whole body. I'm a little nervous here, you see, because instead of just chilling out and thinking about the here and now, I'm thinking about the future for God's sake. And the future consequences of all this. I mean, she seems pretty forward. Things could really happen. Things for which I am not prepared. I mean, never mind my emotional state, I don't have the "famous" condom with me. Yes. My mother, believe it or not, gave me a condom. Which is only slightly embarrassing. She leaves it on my dresser, right? Only slightly embarrassing. 'Cause if I take the thing, she'll know what's up. If I don't take the thing she'll think, poor guy, he's not making it with anybody. If I talk to her about girls, she'll think I'm a pervert, if I don't talk to her about girls she'll think I'm gay. Great! My mother will think I'm gay. But she'll probably think that's cool, because she's such a liberal. Besides, she's always bragging about how "interesting" I am. Then I'd have to break the bad news to her: Sorry Mom, I'm just a plain old ordinary straight guy. Of course my Dad on the other hand doesn't care either way, because the whole idea of sex makes him catatonic, like this . . . *(Stares)* You know, when I look at my parents, I wonder how on earth I was ever conceived. It must have been quite a night. I wonder if it was a night like this one, I think, as I sit here, like a dummy, saying nothing . . . to her, my angel. *(Plays it out with dummies)* Her, saying nothing to me. The silence of a million thoughts passes between us. Who am I kidding? A stupid, awkward silence. *(Pause)* The cost of silence is that nothing is said. The cost of speaking is saying something incredibly STUPID like: *(Blurts out)* "Nice shoes!" Well, I'm nervous, right? And then I start yawning uncontrollably. "Are you tired?" Yeah, I say, I am! Quite tired. Boy, am I tired. (Tired? I won't sleep for two weeks after this!) I gotta go, I say. "What about the Social Studies project? The interview?" Interview? Oh, yeah! "What's it about?" Uh, the cost of living. You know — how much it costs for groceries — what it costs for clothes — how people survive on their salaries. "So — you're not really talking about living at all" she says, "you're talking about surviving. Why don't you really talk about living and what *that* costs? Everybody knows how to survive. But who knows how to live?" Well, I gotta tell you, when she said that, something clicked. Yeah! I'm gonna talk about living. And I'm gonna start by talking about it with her!

> *Now a new image. Interview with* ANGEL, *in which she talks about her feelings. We see a pretty, intelligent, young woman. Probably a little more mature than our guy. But her candidness makes her seem almost naïve, by comparison. She talks freely about teen sexuality, more general than specifically about herself. We see but cannot hear what she says.*

The price of asking someone questions is that they might give you answers. Angel tells me things about herself that I never expect her to say. Never wanted her to say. But she says them. Not bad things. Just things about herself.

Personal things. And suddenly I'm not dealing with a
mannequin anymore, I realize. Or just an idea. But a
person. With feelings. That's the cost of getting to know
someone — you actually get to know them. It's like a
really, really tight close-up of them. Suddenly the idea of
sex becomes . . . how can I explain it . . . ? Intimate . . . and
. . . filled with . . . complications. But that isn't the half
of it.

> *On the screens now are prostitutes on the*
> *streets of Vancouver.*

Sex without cost is not possible, I realize. Because it has
meaning. If it wasn't worth anything, people wouldn't
sometimes pay for it. She says let's go down there, down
where the action is, down there, where light and darkness
meet, secretly in a doorway. That's where the social
studies are. People looking for action . . . for sex without
consequences. And so they exchange money . . . so that
there won't be any other . . . costs. But I don't believe
that's possible anymore. Not since I met Angel. She says
we should go down and find out how they *feel*. Not what
they look like or how much they cost. But how they FEEL.
I never met anyone like this.

Afterwards, we go to a club. Talk about the cost of living.
Clothes. Hair. Shoes. The time consumed, the money. Just
so everybody can stand around...looking good...in the
dark. One lives and breathes hope here. Time stands still
here and waits impatiently, to the beat of the music...for
something...to HAPPEN. Still, Angel wants to know how
everyone feels. Why all this interest in feeling, I ask her?
Instead of answering, she asks — "DO YOU WANT TO
HAVE SEX WITH ME??!!" WHAT!!?? *(In the silence)* "DO

YOU WANT TO HAVE SEX WITH ME!!??" Loud like that. In the middle of the dance floor. People looking at us. It was so weird. *(Music shift)* Outside, we walk along the street without saying a word. Finally I say "Yes, I do as a matter of fact." "That's interesting" she says. And that's the end of that. Another few blocks of silence. "So . . . ?" I says. "So?" That's it? It's interesting. That's it? "Just a coincidence. That's all." Coincidence? "I'd like to have sex with you, too." Oh!! "But I'm not going to." Oh. So why'd she bring it up? Just to make a fool out of me? Why'd she bother mentioning it in the first place? I have a variety of friends with a variety of opinions. The general consensus being that she's basically trying to DRIVE ME CRAZY!!

> *Video. Various clips. People speculating why people do the things they do.*

But these, of course, are guys who don't know Angel. And one woman is not the same as another. Just the way one guy is not the same as another — once you get to know them, and as I said, that's the cost of getting to know someone. You find out that they're just as complicated and screwed up as you are. Even your older people.

To think about *them* as real screwed-up human beings is about the weirdest feeling in the world. Suddenly they're not so big anymore. As a matter of fact, they become sort of small. And everything takes on a slightly different perspective.

But the weirdest feeling of all is to find out, on the eve of my birthday, that the result of my parents' first ever sexual encounter is...the price they pay . . . the cost of their little night of . . . curiosity . . . is . . . me. I was conceived, yes, by two . . . people . . . who didn't know what on earth they were doing. A moment of passion. An accident! So what does that make me? I don't want to think about the philosophical implications at the moment. I don't have time. It is after all the eve of my birthday and I am, after all, going on an official date with Angel. Somewhere very special she says. Knowing Angel, it's bound to be a surprise.

> *With upbeat music, he preps for the big evening.*
> *But rather than himself he uses the dummy.*
> *Dressing it, talking to it, as if he is his own*
> *alter-ego. On the video, meanwhile, men and*
> *women since time (or television) began,*
> *prepping for the big date.*

And just like in the ad, I take the condom, just in case. Mom will want to know everything, but who cares? Wait a minute, dough-head. What are you going to go with this? Just think about this for a second, would you. If and when the happy event should occur, you whip this out, she's going to think it's what you intended all along. She's going to think you're only interested in sex (which you are). She's going to walk away disgusted with you. She'll never want to see you again. *(Going to other ear of dummy)* Yeah, but what about AIDS and all the other sexually transmitted diseases; and what about . . . *pregnancy!*? Isn't it your responsibility — don't you owe it to her and to yourself, and to your mother who will spend the rest of her life wondering why you didn't take the condom when she probably had to go all the way down to the drugstore — no, she probably just borrowed this one from . . . oh my God! This is probably one of Dad's condoms! I can't use this! It'd be like . . . incest or something. *(Now just twisting the head, painfully, back and forth)* On the other hand after all that propaganda at school. On the other hand, what if . . . No. I can't take this thing with me. It's too . . . presumptuous. Besides, isn't it up to the woman? *(Now using female dummy)* After all, she's the one who says yes or no. It wouldn't be so embarrassing for her. Although when you think about it, if she whips one of these out at the magic moment, what's a guy going to think? She's a woman of easy virtue? She has no morals, just like me? Perhaps she's not even a virgin? And she actually WANTS to have sex as much as I do? Besides, how come it's always the woman who gets to say yes or no? What if I want to say yes or no? What if I don't feel like having sex right now, in my delicate state? What if I don't want to go spreading myself around to all and sundry? — oh, right. Sure. You'd like to remain a virgin until the right girl comes along. Right! Like — I happen to LIKE being a virgin — *(Realizing what he said)* not that I am a virgin. That's not what I meant. Not that I care what you think. I *used* to care what you think, but I don't anymore. Not since that night. Because I learned something more that fateful eve of my birthday, but a few short moons ago. Taught to me by a perfect angel, by the name of Angel. A lesson about real love, and the value of human relationships. Sounds heavy, I know. And trust me. It is. But here's me. Preparing for a little light entertainment. Casually dressed for a little casual dinner, afterwards maybe a little casual sex. But as I say — it doesn't quite transpire that way. Angel has other plans. As you may have guessed by now, she's no ordinary girl. And these are no ordinary plans. I'll get to the point, people, but let me first say that she said this was going to be a night worth remembering. So I says, great, I'll bring along my camera. And off I go. *(Picking up dummy)* Just me, myself and I.

111

Recording this momentous evening as I go. I don't want to leave out a single detail. This is, after all, the night of nights. Just like my parents, the night I was . . . you know. Whatever. The symbolism of the evening is not lost on me either, all the similarities of each passing generation. Parents. Grandparents. Same stars. Same beautiful night sky. All the same. Except for two small details. I'm bringing along a camera (thank God my Dad never), and I got a condom with me . . . (also thank God my Dad never) . . . somewhere . . . *(Noticing)* Damn. I can't believe it. I actually left it at home. I'm not going back thank you very much. Just so they can ask *what* I came back for. So I cut over to this drugstore. Establishing shot of me acting cool as I enter.

Ah! People! Shot of me acting cool as I exit.

As I'm walking, to Angel's, I have to tell you, it's like I'm looking at life through a different lens all of a sudden. My whole perspective is changing here. Like, Mr. Video here has been shooting everything in the dark and suddenly someone has turned the lights on. And pow! This is intense scenery. I'm trying capture my feelings here but I can't seem to do it. 'Cause they're a lot bigger than the screen now. Why am I telling you all this? This has got nothing to do with the story. Sorry, sir. I'll get back to the point, shall I? Only I do have to tell you about this one thing that happened to me once. Because I remember it as I'm walking, because my mind is starting to turn over all kinds of things in my life, and I'm looking at them in a different way now, like this time one time I remember. Because I'm rethinking this whole idea about *scoring*, and just wondering why guys talks about sex like sports, with all the back-slapping, shoulder-punching kinda wooah!

kinda parrr-ty, go fer it kinda talk and it reminds me of
this one night last year when me and the boys got together
to do some homework (a popular euphemism for poker),
and we get to talking about the women we've *had*. It's like
this kind of muscle-flexing kind of who scored how many
times, etc. And I can't count the number of women I've
had, since I *haven't* . . . had, up to this point (little bead of
sweat just starting to roll down the side of my temple here,
poker face, keep up the poker face), I am, quite naturally, a
little quiet. Unusual for me. Eventually, of course — all
attention centres on me (Ah, gentlemen), since I have not
yet spoken, and others have already regaled us with their
astonishing sexual exploits. More astonishing since some
of my male friends are about as sophisticated, as charming
as plankton, and about as sexually active. Not to be
outdone, of course, I weave a very elaborate web of lies
about some woman I'd met in . . . Lillooet, I think it was,
never guessing for a minute that someone would actually
be from Lillooet. Whereby I correct myself; not from
Lillooet (did I say from?) Just visiting. Actually . . . from
. . . Hope. (Reflecting more the desire than the place shall
we say.) At any rate, this is a complex tale of an older
woman, as I remember telling it, an English teacher as a
matter of fact . . . and yes . . . her two friends. Stewardesses
. . . from . . . Germany. I won't go into the descriptive
details of this encounter, for fear of appearing a little
exaggerated in my prose style. Suffice it to say, I'm
convincing enough to win the admiration of everyone
around the table, with the exception of a buddy of a
buddy who has been quiet the whole evening. Then — he
looks at all of us and says very calmly: "Those who
actually *do* it don't *talk* about it." A long silence follows.
That pretty well wrecks the evening. Who *is* this guy. A
friend of a friend from across town. A nobody. Why does

everybody hate him so much all of a sudden. Because they know he's right? Anyways — I meet this guy two weeks later at a basketball game. As it turns out he's a big fan of basketball . . . cheerleaders too. I sit down next to him. "That was real cool, what you said. I been thinking about that. From now on I'm not going to talk about the women I have sex with. I'm going to just do it, I'm not going to talk about it. See that cheerleader down there? The red-head? The one I'm having sex with on a regular basis? I'm not going to talk about it." "That cheerleader" he says, "is my girlfriend." Why did I have to say red-head? There was no need to be so specific about it. I won't say he beat me up. Not physically. It was actually worse than that. After the game he drags me over and introduces me to his girlfriend. "I guess you know this guy" he says to her. "No." She says. "Funny" he says. "He seems to know you. In fact . . ." Uh — as a matter of fact, I say — now that I get a closer look . . . I realize I was mistaken. So he takes me aside, grabbing me like this. *(Using dummy)* "A mistake like that could cost someone a lot." "You mean, their *life*?" "No — stupid. Their reputation. I'm talking about her. You ought to have more respect for women, in the future." And he lets me go. And I feel real macho alright. Like a real macho jerk. Suddenly, I want to kill myself. I really do. But I get over it. As you can see. But now every time I hear someone bragging about their amazing sexual encounters, I just say in my coolest voice — those who *do* it don't *talk* about it, and I walk away, in my usual cool fashion. *(Pause)* That guy died. In a car accident. I ran into his girlfriend at a party once. I said "Your boyfriend had a lot of class." But I think she knew that. Geez, you can't do anything anymore. Life is so dangerous — I'm thinking to myself as I'm walking. Can't even drive a car. Can't smoke. Can't eat all kinds of foods. Can't even suntan.

And you certainly can't have sex. Not without thinking about it beforehand. Where's the spontaneity in life? The joie de vivre? I ask myself this daily, but I don't seem to be getting any answers. My grandmother says to me "Oh, you can have fun in all sorts of different ways." Right! Where? In church? Her idea of fun is probably driving her Escort around in the parking lot. Hanging out at the White Spot in the afternoon having a hot time and a Seniors Special with some of her wild friends. There's this guy she hangs out with, and I have to say I actually seen them sort of necking at a Christmas party once. Now *this* . . . is gross. Mostly it's gross because I think — you mean even old people think about sex? You mean I'm going to be like this for the rest of my life? That is — if I'm even *around* for the rest of my life.

Music. Clips of various warnings, from TV, about sex, drinking and driving, etc. There should be a feeling of overwhelming pressure building. To a climax. He cowers. Abruptly it stops.

(*To dummy*) Oh, God. Don't tell me you're here already. At Angel's place, or should I say "the very gates of heaven." Why'd you have to walk so fast? What's the big hurry. Can't you be a little bit cool about this. And why are you so nervous? This is your *big night*. Finally — after all this time. Stop sweating. You wanna smell like a gym class? Push the buzzer. What's your problem? Why are you so stiff all of a sudden? Look at you. Here. Wait. Let me smell your breath. What have you been *eating*!?? Toxic waste!!?? Okay. Relax. It's okay. Just don't open your mouth wide enough to let any air out. Go on. Press the buzzer. One- o- three. Because I'm telling you to. What's your problem? I thought you wanted this. Isn't this what you've been dreaming about since grade seven? What do you mean you're not interested in physical relationships. I see. You're really much more intellectual. Is that it? Some pleasant conversation? Preferably *not* in a reclining position? Forget it. You're going through with this. You know, I never knew this about you. That you were such a prude. This is a new twist. Oh, it's her. It's the idea that you know her. That you like her so much. If only you didn't know her. If only you didn't *like* her. What are you saying? That doesn't make any sense. You'd prefer to have sex with someone you didn't like? You would. So that what? So that you could be cool about the whole thing. It wouldn't matter so much. But then, why would you bother? Why not just hump the side of a building? Well, you see — this is what it costs to have a relationship. You have to actually relate to someone. Like . . . person to person. Dummy. Now, just ring the buzzer.

> *He acts a scene at the front of the apartment building.*

Hi.

Who is it?

(Talk!) It's me. Look. I'm not sure if I can actually go through with this. I like you and everything but I don't think I'm ready for this kind of responsibility. I mean — think of the cost involved. We're human beings we're not just store mannequins. Our lives mean something. Besides, I didn't bring a condom . . . I can't believe it but on top of everything else, I'm not *equipped* to have sex with you — in any way . . . whatsoever . . .

Who *is* this?

It's me. Who's . . . this?

What apartment are you looking for?

Oh, my God.

And if you're not sure about sex — then don't do it.

What?

You're your own person. Do what you want. Don't be pressured.

Look, you just stay out of this, lady. I buzzed the wrong apartment, okay. This happens to be personal. I wanted 103, I got you by mistake.

This *is* 103.

This isn't Angel.

No. It's her mother.

Oh, my God. Oh, my God. Oh, my God. . . .

Would you like to come up?

(Changing his voice) Actually, it's . . . not me . . . it's someone else.

Who is it? Isn't this her date?

Date? Oh, no. God no. It's someone else. *(To dummy)* You idiot! You fool!

He makes the sound of walking away and then footsteps approaching, buzzing the apartment and speaking in his normal voice.

Yes?

Hi. I'm here for Angel.

Weren't you just here?

Oh. You must be talking about the guy I just passed on the sidewalk. Strange-looking dude, yeah. Real uptight. No I'm not him. I'm definitely someone else.

Buzzer sound. Elevator, etc.

What is her mother doing home, I wonder. She never told me about this. One of her surprises. I get to make a fool of myself in front of her mother. Surprise! Besides. If she's home, where are we supposed to . . . have . . . do . . . how are we supposed to . . . what I'm trying to say is . . . vvippp . . . elevator door opens. Tenth floor. I bravely step out. What are you doing on the tenth floor, after all, does she not live on the main floor. Returning to the elevator I press "G" for Gonzo. Goofball. Goober. Gonad. G for g- g-get me out of here. Door opens. Angel is standing there, asking me what I'm doing on the elevator. And naturally I tell her the truth, I was helping an old lady with her groceries. *(Off reaction)* Oh, right. *You* tell the woman of your dreams the ugly, clumsy truth about yourself. Go ahead. I, on the other hand, employ a more sophisticated approach. Tripping on a carpet as I enter, almost toasting a small, but priceless antique vase as I pass it, and greeting the mother with the obligatory spittle on "PPPPleased to meet you." All in all — a brilliant introduction, I'd say. Sweaty palms, stammering, and ah, yes . . . something flying from my pocket, as I go to shake the mother's hand. I see I did, after all, remember the condom. Condom. Condom. Condom. She's very good, I must say. She doesn't even look at it. "I think you've dropped something." "Oh?" And as I quickly stoop to pick it up — an insignificant but rather noisy smashing of the head on the coffee table. *(In pain)* Nothing to worry about. No sooner do I pocket the nasty evidence, when Angel has her coat on and we're out the door. "My mother's *mad* about you." Yeah, right. Mad about me taking her daughter out. By the way — where are we going? What's the big hurry. I thought we were going to be *alone*? This is my special night. "That's right — and I want you to meet someone special. I told him all about you. I told him it was your birthday. He wants to meet you." This is really weird. And getting weirder by the minute. "We're going to be late. Visiting hours are almost over." Visiting hours? We rush through the side entrance of St. Paul's Hospital, down a long hallway, another long hallway, and into an elevator. Whoosh. Up we go. Fssht. Door opens. And down another hallway, another one. A nurse says "Hi, Angel." Another nurse says hello. A guy in a wheelchair waves and smiles. It's like she owns the place. Still, it's not quite my idea of a romantic evening, but clearly this is not what she has in mind. We turn into this room, and it's kind of dark. It never really hits me until now that we're actually in a hospital where sick people are, not until I see this guy, hooked up to all kinds of stuff. He must weigh eighty pounds, like nothing there, just skin and bones and a little pair of watery eyes and smiling. "Hello," he says. Really weak, right. "Hello — you must be the guy Angel told me about. Happy Birthday."

I shook his hand and it was so small. Then Angel leaves the room for a minute to go *talk* to someone. Nice move, Angel. And I'm stuck here, with a goofball smile on my face, thinking — no — don't leave me in here alone with this sick guy. I feel like such a dope. I don't know what to say. I'm freaking out here. Of course naturally I have to open my big mouth.

"I guess you're pretty sick, huh?" (Oh — nice dialogue!)

"Yeah, it's AIDS-related" he says. "I guess she didn't tell you."

(No she tends to leave out the trivial details.) "No" I said, "she didn't tell me." (This is unbelievable! *This* is Angel's birthday surprise?)

"I was hoping I'd meet you — Angel thinks you're pretty special. And any friend of Angel's is a friend of mine. By the way" he says "I'd like to give you some friendly advice. Think of it as a birthday offering."

Yeah — right. Where the hell is Angel? Tight shot on me. Goofball expression. "So, uh . . . how do you know Angel?"

"It's a long story" he says.

Right. "So uh . . . what's the advice?"

"Don't ever . . . ever . . . wear that shirt with that tie."

Stunned reaction shot. "Excuse me?"

"They don't go together. That's my advice."

"That's it? That's you're advice?"

"What were you looking for?" he says.

"Well, I don't know. I thought maybe . . . you were going to give me some lecture about safe sex or something."

"You look like an adult to me" he says. "I don't need to tell you how to survive. Besides" he says, "*I ought to be warning enough for you.* After all, you see someone get hit by a car — you start looking both ways before you cross the street. Unfortunately, in my case, nobody even told me there was a road there."

Here's me. Just staring at him. You see, what I couldn't fathom was how he was taking all this so normally. We didn't say anything for the longest time, and then finally, he fell asleep. He's not dead or anything, but he sure looks like he's going to be. Then Angel comes in. Takes my hand. Now we're both just standing there.

Pause.

"Ready to go?" — she says, like we been hanging out in a mall or something.

Yeah, I'm ready to go. Ready to go insane from this nightmare. Finally we get out of the hospital and down

121

into the street where I can breathe some air. We walk forever without saying anything. Then out of the blue she says "He's got AIDS. I assume you know all about that." Not really very much I say. Inside though I'm going crazy. I know you can't get it from shaking hands or anything but all the same. My hands . . . hands . . . sweat . . . disease, virus. It's the idea. I wish she'd told me. But then — there's a lot she hasn't told me. Not in so many words. So I ask her: "Why'd you take me there?"

"He knows a lot about life" she says, "probably more than you and I will ever know. He knows what it can cost. You wanna do a real essay, do one on him."

Now a time shift. Cross fade to a scene on the beach. Me and Angel, some moments later, sitting on a log. Looking out over the water. There's no one else around, just our voices lifting up over the sand like seagulls. Thoughts flying around, swooping, diving. The sun is disappearing and the stars are just beginning to peek through at us, and I slowly realize, almost imperceptibly, we are alone together and now is the time. This is all so unplanned. I mean, like this. Out of control. Hands. Lips. Eyes. Yes, there seems to be a birthday party developing here. Surprise! And developing here, and here, and around the collar, here — button by button, down my shirt . . . incidentally — what's wrong with this shirt? Who is this guy, Angel? And what's his connection to you? They used to live together, she tells me. Last semester, when they started college. But he got sick. Live together??? As in lovers? As in pelvic affiliates? As in the exchange of bodily fluids — on a continual basis? As in — as in — as in — why am I lying here on this beach...doing mouth to mouth with . . . lovers . . . sort of? Surprise!! Wait a second. He's gay, right? I'm asking, but she's not answering. It's gay people who get AIDS, right? Anybody can get AIDS — she says — it's a disease. It doesn't play favorites. All you have to be is human. And unlucky. I look at her. Zoom right in on those beautiful Angel eyes. I don't know what to say. I look at her. I can't *believe* . . . I want to ask . . . I *have* to ask . . . I ask . . . do *you* have . . . uh, do *you*, . . . *did* you . . . did *he* . . . did the *both* of you . . . ? Does he . . . ? . . . *Is* he . . . ? *Was* he . . . were *you* . . . are you? . . . do you . . .

"Do I have AIDS?"

Uh, yeah . . . I was sort of wondering . . .

"I don't know, really" she says. "I suppose there's a mathematical possibility . . . but aren't you sort of missing the point, here?"

Oh! There' s a *point* to all this!

"Life" she says, "is filled with mathematical possibilities. The possibility that we met for example. And the odds that we liked each other. And what about the odds on my friend in the hospital? What do you suppose are his chances for the future? What are the mathematical possibilities that *he* would get AIDS and others wouldn't? That's what life is all about. A collision of possibilities. Accidents. But you don't think so — do you? You don't think it's possible for you to get AIDS because you think you're somehow superior."

"Wait a second." I'm getting mad here! "I don't think I'm superior."

But she doesn't stop.

"You have this idea that life is some kind of TV show and you're the central character. You look at the world through a camera and you expect everything to fall neatly into place. Boy meets girl. No complications. But the truth is bigger than a TV screen. It includes all the possibilities."

"What are you getting on *my* case for?" I can see her eyes welling up with tears. "I'm just afraid."

Anyway — we have this fight. I don't know what it's about. It's about a minute and a half. That's what it's about. And off she goes. Into the night. And I'm still missing the point. So — this is my birthday gift from Angel. A night to remember. This ugly little scene in the moonlight. I sit back down. And I am just like this total . . . I wonder if they make any condoms for a dick as big as me. What's this? She dropped this card in the sand. Looks like a birthday card. "You'll find you gift," it says, "hidden beneath the stars." *(Pause to consider)* It takes me a while — I'm kinda slow. I didn't figure it out till a few days later. I realize she's talking about life . . . everything . . . the whole world . . . and my place in it. Life is a gift. That's why she took me to see her friend. The gift was just being with him. Feeling how much life meant to him as he was slowly slipping away from it. A feeling, now that I have it, I will never surrender. A feeling that made me do this essay the way I'm doing it. Sharing my sense of the world with you. About its calamities and joys. Its ugliness, its poverty, its wealth and its beauty. Its sicknesses like AIDS. Those are the cost of living. In fact, the cost of living is enormous. It cost me my youth, my ignorance, my girl-friend, it'll probably cost me my Social Studies grade. But it hasn't cost me my life, yet. And I don't intend it to. A healthy respect for sex is a good place to start, I figure. Like Angel's friend said: "Looking both ways before you cross the street." My new common sense approach to life, along with a new tie. The other one didn't go with the shirt, remember? Actually, I think he was talking about something else. My attitude. I think it was, like, a metaphor. Tie . . . attitude . . . tie . . . you get the picture. This is the picture. Action shot of me — life-size — getting my life into focus. I don't have to have what everybody else has any longer. Don't have to be what everybody else is. Don't have to feel what everybody else feels. There's just me. Feeling what I feel. Being what I am. Lost. Confused. In love.

Music up and out.

THE END